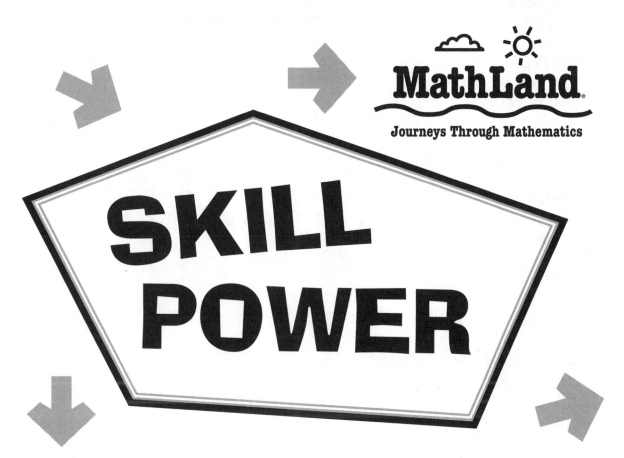

MathLand

Journeys Through Mathematics

SKILL POWER

Essential Practice for Every Day

Homework

Arithmetic Practice

Problem Solving

GRADE 5

Test Practice

Vocabulary

Creative Publications

Writers
Julie Pier Brodie
Rhea Irvine
Mary Kirsch
Cynthia Reak
Ann Roper
Kelly Stewart
Kathryn Walker
Meg Velez

Project Editors
Jo Dennis
Cynthia Reak
Andy Strauss
Kristin Ferraioli

Editors
Jane Books
Ann Roper

Cover Design
Joslyn Hidalgo

Production Coordinator
Ed Lazar

Editorial Development
Pubworks

Production
Morgan-Cain & Associates

Portions of this book were previously published
under the title *Daily Tune-Ups II*.

Wright Group/McGraw-Hill
One Prudential Plaza
Chicago, IL 60601
www.WrightGroup.com
Customer service: 800-624-0822

Printed in the United States of America
ISBN 0-7622-0453-2
   3 4 5 6 7 8 9 10 MAL 10 09 08 07 06

Contents

Guidebook		Introduction	Vocabulary	Estimation	Computation Review	"Convince Me!"	Problems	Practice Tests
1	Data	1	2, 3	8	13	14	4-7 9-12	15, 16
2	Patterns	17	18, 19	24	29	30	20-23 25-28	31, 32
3	Strategies	33	34, 35	40 55	45 60	50	36-39 41-44 46-49 51-54 56-59	61, 62
4	Sets	63	64, 65	75	76	70	66-69 71-74	77, 78
5	Millions	79	80, 81	91 106	96	86 101	82-85 87-90 92-95 97-100 102-105	107, 108
6	Volume and Capacity	109	110, 111	126	116	121	112-115 117-120 122-125	127, 128
7	Fractions	129	130,131	146	136 151	141 156	132-135 137-140 142-145 147-150 152-155	157, 158
8	Geometry	159	160, 161	166 181	171 182	176	162-165 167-170 172-175 177-180	183, 184
9	Number Systems	185	186, 187	197 208	202	192 207	188-191 193-196 198-201 203-206	209, 210
10	Probability	211	212, 213		218	223	214-217 219-222	224 225

Dear Student,

Skill Power is a collection of challenging arithmetic problems that may be used for class work or homework. There are some special pages that will help you practice and review mental computation ("Convince Me!"), estimation, and test-taking skills.

You'll begin each unit by learning or reviewing a few vocabulary terms and then using the words for a puzzle or an activity. During the year, you'll be solving different types of problems. After solving a problem, you are often asked to "show your thinking." That means you need to explain how you got your answer. Other questions ask how solving one problem can help you solve similar problems. Use a separate piece of paper so you have enough space to draw or write about your thinking. (Sometimes your teacher may ask you to show your thinking for just one problem.)

Even when there is only one correct answer to a problem, there may be many different ways to find that answer. Talk with your classmates about how you figured out the answers. You'll learn how to convince them your thinking is correct. Listen to their ideas. You'll probably learn other ways to solve a problem!

If you are using *Skill Power* for homework, share your thinking with your family as you solve the problems. Remember, good thinking takes time!

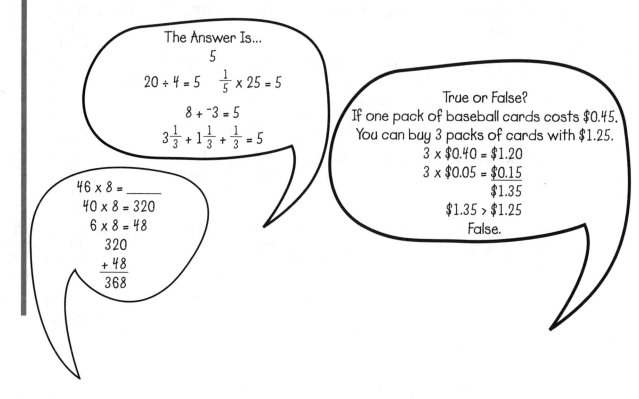

Dear Family,

The arithmetic problems in *Skill Power* focus on building number sense. Students are asked not only to get the correct answers, but also to explain their thinking. This emphasis on reasoning skills gives children a strong arithmetic base. These exercises also include multiple-choice and true/false problems to prepare students for the format and language they might see on tests.

To encourage good thinking, most problems ask the student to prove an answer or tell about his or her reasoning. While there is usually one correct answer to a problem, there may be many different strategies or ways to arrive at that answer. The more strategies students develop, the more efficient and confident they become as problem solvers.

You will probably find it interesting to work with your child as he or she works in *Skill Power*. Express your appreciation for the effort and thinking your child shows and for the explanations he or she writes. If your child makes an error, instead of saying "wrong" or telling the correct answer, help your child to rethink the answer.

Here is a sample of an actual response to a typical problem for the fifth grade. The emphasis is on having students find correct solution methods that make sense to them, and also to explain or show their thinking.

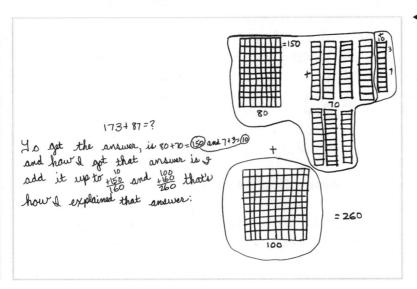

◄ This student's strategy was to add the tens first, then the ones, and finally to add the hundreds for a total of 260. He also included a sketch to illustrate and to support his solution.

Dear Student and Family,

The problems in *Skill Power* probably look like other problems you have seen before, but the way you solve the problems might be different from what you are used to doing. Below are examples of *MathLand* problems and students' thinking in solving them.

"Convince Me!"

You will use the "Convince Me!" method to solve many of the problems in *Skill Power*. After you calculate an answer, you explain *how* you solved the problem, convincing others that the answer is correct!
Example: The problem is 427 − 219 = _____.

Otis' solution:
"The answer is 208."
$$400 - 200 = 200$$
$$27 - 20 = \underline{7}$$
$$207 + 1 = 208$$

Ginny's solution:
"The answer is 208."

427	428
− 219	− 220
	208

Estimation

There are two types of estimation pages in *Skill Power* to help you build your estimation skills. Estimating before you work a problem lets you know if an answer is reasonable. What are other reasons for estimating an answer?

On "It's Between" pages, you will write two estimates, one that is less than and one that is greater than the actual answer.
Example: 527 + 279 is between <u>800</u> and <u>850</u> .
Why? 525 + 275 = 800; 550 + 300 = 850; 527 is between 525 and 550; 279 is between 275 and 300, so the answer is between 800 and 850.
On "Greater Than, Less Than" pages, you will estimate whether an answer would be greater than (>) or less than (<) a given answer.
Example: 382 + 461 is <u>less</u> than 900 because 400 + 500 = 900; 382 + 461 is less than 400 + 500, so 382 + 461 is less than 900.

Computation Review

These are mixed-practice pages for reviewing your computation skills. Try to solve each of the 20 problems as quickly as you can. You don't need to explain your thinking, but comparing solution methods with your classmates may give you some new strategies to use next time!

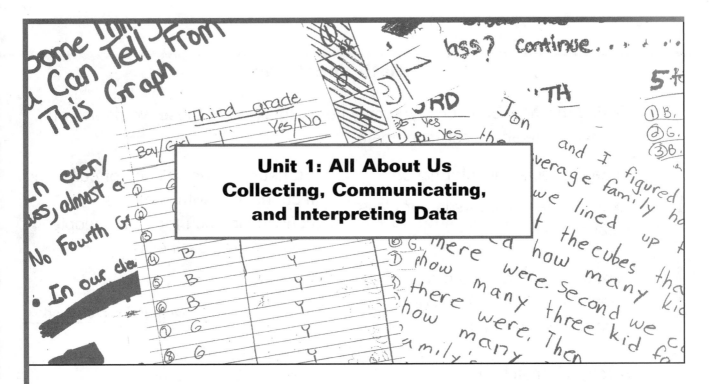

Unit 1: All About Us
Collecting, Communicating, and Interpreting Data

Thinking Questions

What is the average number of children in the families of the students in your class? What is the average number of pets in a family? How could you conduct a survey? How could you use the results?

Investigations

In this MathLand unit, you will discover answers to these questions and more as your class collects data and creates graphs and diagrams to report that data. You will learn how to interpret the information on a display of data, and you will investigate ways in which surveys can be used to make decisions about many things.

Real-World Math

Watch for different ways data displays are used in everyday life. Some examples that you might see in the newspaper are weather reports, sports statistics, advertisements comparing products, and reports of the results of scientific studies. In what other ways do you see data being used?

Math Vocabulary

During this MathLand unit, you may be using some of these words as you talk and write about collecting data.

Data are facts and information.

Example: Ten students in our class wear braces.

A **poll** is a survey of a group of people to get information or to record their opinions.

A **tally** is a notch or mark to represent a number.

Example: Put a tally mark beside your choice of sandwich.

Tuna	///
Cheese	/////

A **sample** is a small group used to predict what a larger group likes.

Example: A clothing company surveyed a sample fifth-grade class to find out which products were most popular.

Statistics is the science of collecting facts dealing with numbers concerning such topics as people, weather, and business.

Example:

City	Average Precipitation
Portland	44 in.
Rapid City	17 in.
Houston	46 in.

A **Venn diagram** is a diagram of overlapping circles that show how data are related.

Swim Strokes People Can Do

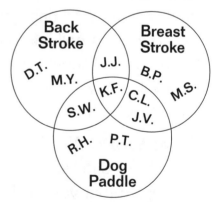

Data Dig

Find each word from the word bank in the block of letters.
Words may go up, down, across, backward, or diagonally.
When you finish, cross out all the z's you did not use.
To answer the riddle, write all the letters you did not use on the lines, in order, starting at the upper left-hand corner.

Word Bank

add
analysis
average
collect
comparisons
count
data
diagram
graph
interpret
poll
sample
sampling
set
statistics
survey
surveying
tally
Venn diagram

A	V	Z	G	N	I	L	P	M	A	S	C	L
S	Z	E	Z	D	D	A	T	Z	N	L	O	S
N	A	C	N	S	E	T	A	D	A	B	L	U
O	T	O	O	N	U	T	L	A	L	E	L	R
S	E	U	Z	Z	D	Z	L	T	Y	G	E	V
I	R	N	Z	Z	Z	I	Y	A	S	A	C	E
R	P	T	E	L	P	M	A	S	I	R	T	Y
A	R	P	O	L	L	Z	Z	G	S	E	Z	I
P	E	Z	S	U	R	V	E	Y	R	V	Z	N
M	T	Z	Z	Z	D	I	A	G	R	A	M	G
O	N	Z	G	R	A	P	H	Z	U	Z	M	Z
C	I	S	T	A	T	I	S	T	I	C	S	S

This unit is ___ ___ ___   ___ ___ ___ ___ ___   ___ ___!

Name _____

1

Write the Answers

371 + 128 = _____

361 + 138 = _____

261 + 238 = _____

Explain your thinking.

2

Choose the Correct Answer

6 × 4 has the same answer as
which of the following?

A   7 × 3

B   8 × 4

C   12 × 2

D   9 × 3

Tell how you know.

3

Can You Buy a Granola Bar?

If you have $0.35 and your friend
has $0.58, do both of you
together have enough money to
buy one granola bar that costs
$0.89? Would you have any
money left over?

Explain how you know.

4

True or False?

247 − 226 < 389 − 368

406 − 201 > 617 − 411

578 − 367 < 985 − 754

If any statements are false,
change them to true statements.

1

Write the Answers

516 − 82 = _____

514 − 80 = _____

792 − 45 = _____

797 − 50 = _____

Explain your thinking.

Write another set of problems like these.

2

Choose the Correct Answer

9 in. + 14 in. + 25 in. = _____

A   38 in.

B   3 ft 9 in.

C   4 ft

D   4 ft 3 in.

Tell how you know.

3

Solve

Robbie read 125 pages of his book in 5 d. If he read the same number of pages each day, how many pages did he read in 2 d?

Show your work.

4

Which Is Greater?

Put < or > in each circle to show which is greater.

$\frac{1}{3}$ of 18   ◯ $\frac{1}{4}$ of 20

$\frac{1}{2}$ of 18   ◯ $\frac{1}{2}$ of 20

$\frac{1}{3}$ of 24   ◯ $\frac{1}{4}$ of 24

Show how you know.

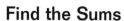

1

Find the Sums

$$
\begin{array}{r} 748 \\ +\ 37 \\ \hline \end{array}
\qquad
\begin{array}{r} 745 \\ +\ 40 \\ \hline \end{array}
$$

$$
\begin{array}{r} 692 \\ +\ 29 \\ \hline \end{array}
\qquad
\begin{array}{r} 691 \\ +\ 30 \\ \hline \end{array}
$$

Explain your thinking.

Write another set of problems like these.

2

Choose the Correct Answer

Which two numbers have a difference of 27?

A   45 and 62

B   89 and 52

C   141 and 113

D   682 and 709

Tell how you know.

3

The Answer Is 12

Write at least 6 different equations that have this answer.

4

Share With 3 Friends

Mai has 94 little candies that she wants to share equally with 3 friends. How many pieces of candy will each person get?

Explain how you know.

Cat Food

This display shows 7 flavors of the best-selling treats at The Cat's Gourmet.
The circular display holds tuna-flavored treats.
The square display holds turkey-flavored treats.
The rectangular display holds cheese-flavored treats.

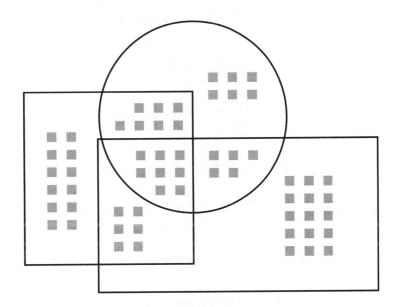

1. How many treats are just tuna flavored?

2. How many treats are just turkey flavored?

3. How many treats are just cheese flavored?

4. How many treats are tuna-cheese flavored?

5. How many treats are turkey-cheese flavored?

6. How many treats are tuna-turkey flavored?

7. Mr. Washington's cat, Sam, will eat anything but cheese.
How many treats are not cheese flavored?

8. Finicky Fiona will not eat turkey. How many treats are not turkey flavored?

9. Ms. Gomez won't let her cat, Charlie, eat tuna. How many
treats are not tuna flavored?

10. Mrs. Lui's Siamese cat loves the tuna-turkey-cheese combination.
How many of these treats are there?

What's a Good Estimate?
Greater Than, Less Than

Build your estimation skills. For each problem, tell if the answer will be
less than (<) or greater than (>) the estimate given. Explain why you think so.

1. 382 + 461 is _____ than 900 because _____

_____

2. $0.68 + $0.21 is _____ than $0.80 because _____

_____

3. $\frac{1}{4}$ of 19 is _____ than 5 because _____

_____

4. 836 − 218 is _____ than 600 because _____

_____

5. 81 ÷ 4 is _____ than 20 because _____

_____

Now, make up your own problem like one on this page.

▼ **PARENT NOTE:**
Strong estimation skills are important. Estimating before, during and after calculating
the exact answer is one way students can check themselves as they work.

1

Write the Answers

274 + 19 = _____

273 + 20 = _____

689 + 27 = _____

686 + 30 = _____

Tell how you know.

Write another set of problems like these.

2

What Is the Average Score?

The scores for Green School's last 6 baseball games were: 5, 7, 0, 4, 2, and 6. What is the team's average score for the 6 games?

Explain your thinking.

3

What's Your Story?

Write a story problem using the numbers 4, 6, and 24. Write the solution for the problem.

Explain how you know.

4

True or False?

19 − 11 = 29 − 21

46 − 13 = 56 − 33

82 − 21 = 92 − 11

58 − 24 = 78 − 44

If any statements are false, change them to true ones.

1

Write the Answers

$$\begin{array}{r} 13 \\ \times\ 6 \\ \hline \end{array} \qquad \begin{array}{r} 26 \\ \times\ 3 \\ \hline \end{array}$$

$$\begin{array}{r} 27 \\ \times\ 8 \\ \hline \end{array} \qquad \begin{array}{r} 54 \\ \times\ 4 \\ \hline \end{array}$$

Explain your thinking.

Write another set of problems like these.

2

Choose the Correct Answer

What coins make 43¢?

A   1 quarter, 2 nickels, 3 pennies

B   1 quarter, dime, nickel, 3 pennies

C   2 dimes, 3 nickels, 2 pennies

D   3 dimes, 3 nickels, 2 pennies

Explain how you know.

3

Newspaper by the Pound

The fifth-grade classes are recycling newspapers. Room 12 collected 265 pounds, Room 13 collected 328 pounds, and Room 14 collected 287 pounds. How many pounds did the classes collect all together?

Tell how you know.

4

True or False?

If one pack of baseball cards costs $0.45, you can buy 3 packs of cards with $1.25.

Explain your answer.

1

Solve

$$7 \overline{)168} \qquad 7 \overline{)84}$$

$$8 \overline{)144} \qquad 8 \overline{)72}$$

$$9 \overline{)396} \qquad 9 \overline{)198}$$

Explain your thinking.

2

Choose the Correct Answer

$$\begin{array}{r} 159 \\ -132 \\ \hline \end{array}$$

A   81

B   27

C   37

D   32

Tell how you know.

3

The Answer Is 25

Write at least 8 equations that have this answer.

4

Agree or Disagree?

Manuel said that $\frac{4}{8}$ has the same value as $\frac{1}{2}$.

Explain your answer.

PARENT NOTE:
Learning to communicate one's thinking and to consider other students' strategies are skills that students will develop throughout the year as they write about and discuss their ways of solving math problems.

Favorite Pet

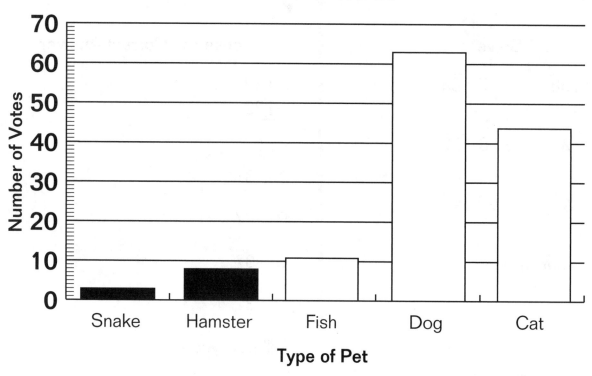

Ms. Tran's fifth-grade class asked other fifth graders in their school what their favorite pet was. Finish the graph. Answer the questions.

There were 3 more votes for Fish than for Hamster.
There were 21 times as many votes for Dog as there were for Snake.
There were 19 fewer votes for Cat than there were for Dog.

1. What type of pet got the most votes? How many votes did it get?
2. How many more votes for Cat than for Fish were there?
3. How many fewer votes for Snake than for Dog were there?
4. How many students voted in the survey?

▼ **PARENT NOTE:**
One goal of these pages is for students to build strong mental computation skills. Choose a few questions and ask your child to tell you how she or he solved them.

What's an Easy Way?
Computation Review

Solve these problems as quickly as you can. Use the strategies that work best for you.

Add.

1. 20 + 70

2. 340 + 110

3. 640 + 210

4. 45 + 30

5. 78 + 10

6. 37 + 50

7. 35 + 45

8. 61 + 18

9. 23 + 47

Solve.

10. 26 + 32

11. 17×2

12. $123 \div 5$

13. 436 + 345

14. 538 − 127

15. 27×4

16. $154 \div 7$

17. 512 − 371

18. 73×5

19. 354 − 203

20. $186 \div 9$

▼ PARENT NOTE:
We live in an information-rich society. Mental computation is a necessary skill because we see or hear much of the number information we receive.

What's Your Strategy?
Convince Me!

Otis and Ginny each solved the problem 427 − 219 = _____. Look at their solutions. Notice that Otis and Ginny got the same, correct answer, but they used different strategies.

Otis explained his strategy.
The teacher recorded it for the class this way:

Ginny explained her strategy.
The teacher recorded it for the class this way:

$$427 - 219 = \underline{\quad}$$

$$400 - 200 = 200$$
$$30 - 19 = \underline{\;11}$$
$$211 - 3 = 208$$

$$427 - 219 = \underline{\quad}$$

$$\begin{array}{r} 427 \\ -219 \\ \hline \end{array} \qquad \begin{array}{r} 428 \\ -220 \\ \hline 208 \end{array}$$

Solve the problems below. Record your explanation on paper.

1. 95 − 79 = _____

2. 84 − 68 = _____

3. 615 − 309 = _____

4. 996 − 577 = _____

5. 741 − 328 = _____

6. 822 − 609 = _____

▼—PARENT NOTE:
On this page, students solve problems much as they do in class Convince Me! discussions: they use their own thinking and also see other students' strategies for solving arithmetic problems.

A Trip to the Corner Store

Fill in the bubble next to the correct answer.

1. Which shows the prices of these items listed from least to greatest?

- ○ **A.** key chain, comic book, baseball cards, ball
- ○ **B.** comic book, key chain, baseball cards, ball
- ○ **C.** ball, baseball cards, key chain, comic book
- ○ **D.** ball, baseball cards, comic book, key chain.

2. Terry bought one of each of these items. How much change did he get from $10.00.

- ○ **A.** $1.51
- ○ **C.** $2.51
- ○ **B.** $1.61
- ○ **D.** $2.61

3. Joella bought 3 packs of baseball cards and a comic book. How much did she spend in all?

- ○ **A.** $3.75
- ○ **C.** $6.74
- ○ **B.** $4.24
- ○ **D.** $12.72

4. Steve has $4. How many balls can he buy?

- ○ **A.** 3
- ○ **C.** 5
- ○ **B.** 4
- ○ **D.** 6

5. Emily has $5 and buys a comic book. What other items could she buy?

- ○ **A.** ball only
- ○ **B.** ball and baseball cards
- ○ **C.** baseball cards only
- ○ **D.** either ball or baseball cards, but not both

The Bake Sale

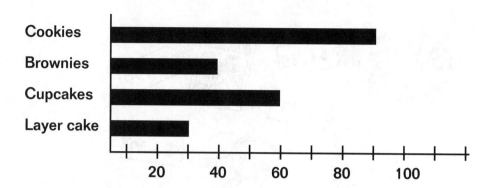

1. How many cookies were sold at the bake sale?

2. List the items in order from least number sold to greatest number sold.

3. Brownies sold for $0.50 each. How much money did they collect from selling brownies?

4. The bake sale started at 3:15 pm and continued for one and one-half hours. When was the bake sale over?

5. Amy brought 24 cupcakes to the sale arranged in rows in a box. If each row had the same number, what are the possible arrangements of cupcakes in the box?

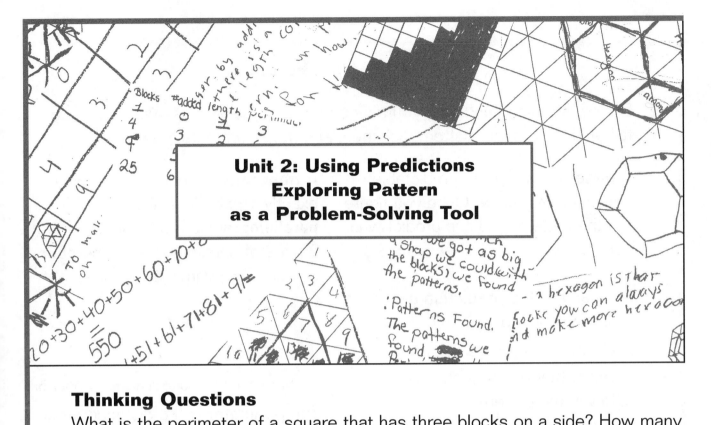

Thinking Questions

What is the perimeter of a square that has three blocks on a side? How many blocks do you need to cover the square? How many more blocks do you need to cover a square with four blocks on a side? What is the perimeter of the new square? How can you use patterns to solve these problems?

Investigations

In this MathLand unit, you will discover the answers to these questions and more as your class uses patterns to solve problems. You will explore geometric shapes and use patterns to make predictions about other shapes. You will also discover patterns in solutions to simple problems and then use them to solve more difficult ones.

Real-World Math

Notice how patterns occur in everyday life. Some patterns are used by artists to create designs. Other patterns are used by scientists to predict events such as changes in the weather and the path of a meteor. The pattern of the seasons is a part of our lives and is celebrated in different ways in every culture. What patterns can you find in your daily routine?

Math Vocabulary

During this MathLand unit, you may be using some of these words as you talk and write about patterns, shapes, and measurements.

A **pattern** is a regular, predictable design or sequence. Once you figure out the pattern, you can predict what comes next.

You can make a **prediction** based on what you know or observe.

Example: △○▽△○▽ is a pattern. I predict that the next shapes to follow in the pattern are △○▽△○▽ .

A **polygon** is a closed, flat figure with 3 or more sides.

polygons   not polygons

A **quadrilateral** is a polygon with four sides. A **pentagon** is a polygon with five sides. A **hexagon** is a polygon with six sides.

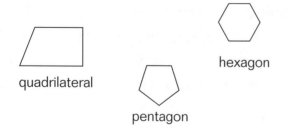

quadrilateral

pentagon

hexagon

A **trapezoid** is a quadrilateral with exactly 1 pair of parallel sides. A **parallelogram** is a quadrilateral with 2 pairs of parallel sides. A **rhombus** is a parallelogram with all sides of equal length.

trapezoid   parallelogram   rhombus

The **perimeter** is the distance around the edges of an object or shape.

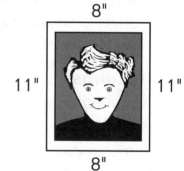

Perimeter = 8" + 8" + 11" + 11"
Perimeter = 38"

A **square number** is the product of a number multiplied by itself.

Examples: 25 = 5 × 5; 36 = 6 × 6

Name _____

Scrambled Shapes

Unscramble the vocabulary words.

Write the letter that matches each word to its example on the right side of the paper.

1. N G P E O N T A

○ _ _ _ _ _ _ _   _ _

2. G P L N O O Y

_ ○ _ _ _ _ _   _ _

3. T R E I M E R P E

_ _ _ _ _ _ ○ _ _   _

4. U O S B H R M

_ ○ _ _ _ _ _   _ _

5. X E A G N O H

_ ○ _ _ _ _ _   _ _

6. Q S R E U A   R B M U N E

○ _ _ _ _ _   _ _ _ _ _ _   _ _

7. E I O P D R T Z A

_ _ _ _ _ _ _ _ _   _ _

8. R T P E A T N

_ ○ _ _ _ _ _   _ _

9. N O R P E C I I T D

_ _ _ _ _ _ _ _ _ _   _ _

10. L L L P R G A A A E O M R

_ _ _ _ _ _ _ _ _ _ _ _ _   _ _

11. T E R I R Q A A A U L D L

_ ○ _ _ _ _ _ _ _ _ _ _   _ _

A. ◇

B. 3" □ 3" = 12" (3" top, 3" bottom)

C. 4 = 2 × 2

D. ▱

E. ▱

F. ⬿

G. ⬠

H. ⬡

I. The sky is dark; I bet it rains today.

J. □○□○□○□

K. ▱ (trapezoid)

Arrange the letters in the circles above to find the answer to the riddle.

What did the Square reply when the Rectangle asked why he was at the gym?

"I'm a little _ _ _ of _ _ _ _ _."

© Creative Publications

Skill Power • 5   **19**

Name _____

Subtract

82 − 28 = _____

84 − 30 = _____

91 − 39 = _____

92 − 40 = _____

Explain your thinking.

Write another set of problems like these.

Choose the Correct Answer

Which has an answer of 25?

A   12 + 8 + 6

B   5 × 5 × 0

C   3 × 7 + 4

D   5 × 5 − 1

Tell how you know.

What Is the Average?

Hyru rode her bike 12 blocks on Monday, 15 blocks on Tuesday, 6 blocks on Friday, and 15 blocks on Saturday. What is the average number of blocks she rode each day?

Explain your answer.

Which Is Greater?

Put < or > in each circle to show which is greater.

14 × 7 ◯ 15 × 6

23 × 8 ◯ 24 × 9

16 × 5 ◯ 19 × 4

Show how you know.

PARENT NOTE:
Arithmetic problems in *Skill Power* are designed to develop strong mental computation and estimation skills, developing students' ability to handle numbers in many ways.

Find the Sum

```
  439
+  66
```

Explain your thinking.

Choose the Best Answer

473 − 69

A   The answer is about 300.

B   The answer is exactly 314.

C   The answer is about 400.

D   The answer is exactly 416.

Tell how you know.

How Many Red Jelly Beans Are There?

Carrie has 14 jelly beans in her bag. One-half of them are red. How many red jelly beans does she have?

Explain how you know.

True or False?

If 1 pound of oranges costs $0.39, then 5 pounds of oranges cost $1.85.

Explain your answer.

1

Subtract

598 − 29 = _____

Explain how you know.

2

Choose the Correct Answer

Which two numbers have
a sum of 476?

A   298 and 278

B   327 and 149

C   428 and 58

D   356 and 220

Tell how you know.

3

The Answer Is 8

Write at least 6 subtraction
equations that have this answer.

4

Which Square Takes More Tiles?

Julia covered a square area with
tiles, putting 9 tiles along each
side. Kevin did the same, putting
6 tiles on each side. Which square
took more tiles to make? How
many more tiles did it take?

Explain your answer.

Tabatha's Tiles

Tabatha's Tile Company puts in tiles. The most popular tile pattern is shown.

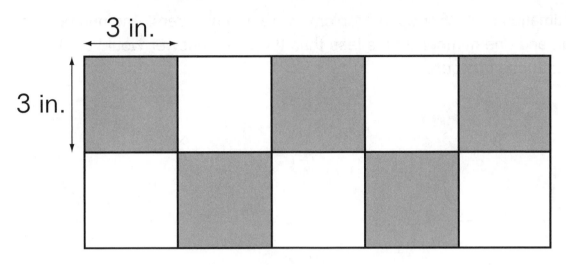

How many light tiles should Tabatha order for the following areas?

1. 30 in. by 30 in. area _____   **3.** 15 in. by 15 in. area _____

2. 24 in. by 24 in. area _____   **4.** 36 in. by 15 in. area _____

Tabatha ordered the following number of light tiles. What are the dimensions of the area that will fit tiles in this pattern?

5. 18 light tiles _____   **7.** 36 light tiles _____

6. 27 light tiles _____   **8.** 12 light tiles _____

Tabatha ordered the following number of light tiles. How many dark tiles should she order? What are the dimensions of the area?

9. 10 light tiles _____   **10.** 20 light tiles _____

What's a Good Estimate?
It's Between ...

Build your estimation skills. For each problem, write two numbers, one number that is greater than and one number that is less than the exact answer would be. Explain why you chose those numbers.

$$527 + 279$$

$$46 \times 4$$

_____ and _____   _____ and _____

Why? _____   Why? _____

_____   _____

$$831 - 428 = \underline{\hspace{1cm}}$$

$$94 \div 6 = \underline{\hspace{1cm}}$$

_____ and _____   _____ and _____

Why? _____   Why? _____

_____   _____

William wants to buy 6 bottles of fruit punch for his party. Each bottle costs $2.79. How much will the fruit punch cost?

William needs between $_____ and $_____ for the punch.

Why? _____

▼ **PARENT NOTE:**
Students often clarify their thinking as they explain it. Take time
to read or listen and respond to your child's explanations.

Find the Sums

```
 42      25
 63      31
+12     +72
___     ___


 27      18
 14      24
+23     +52
___     ___
```

Explain your solutions.

Choose the Correct Answer

80 × 7 = _____

A   490

B   640

C   567

D   560

Tell how you know.

The School Fair

Sai bought 50 tickets to go on rides at the school fair. If each ride takes 3 tickets, how many rides can Sai go on?

Explain how you know.

True or False?

12 quarters = 30 dimes

8 quarters = 20 dimes

45 dimes = 9 nickels

If any statements are false, change them to true ones.

1

Write the Answers

$\frac{1}{2}$ of 32 = _____

$\frac{1}{4}$ of 32 = _____

$\frac{1}{4}$ of 16 = _____

$\frac{1}{2}$ of 16 = _____

Which equation did you solve first? Did you use that solution to solve the other equations? If so, how?

2

Choose the Correct Answer

4 ft 3 in. − 2 ft 9 in. = _____

A   2 ft 6 in.

B   15 in.

C   1 ft 6 in.

D   1 ft 9 in.

Show your thinking.

3

How Much Money Will She Have?

Stacy's allowance increases by $1.00 each week. If she gets $3.00 the first week, how much will she get on the fourth week? On the eighth week? If she saves her money, how much will she have all together after 8 weeks?

Explain your answer.

4

Which Is Greater?

Put < or > in each circle to show which is greater.

$\frac{1}{3}$ of 12 ◯ $\frac{1}{2}$ of 10

$\frac{1}{3}$ of 24 ◯ $\frac{1}{2}$ of 20

$\frac{1}{3}$ of 18 ◯ $\frac{1}{2}$ of 15

Tell how you know.

▼ **PARENT NOTE:**
Students are often interested in doing problems like number 3 above that relate to their own experiences. It is important that students explain their answers. Encourage your child to tell how he or she got the answer.

Find the Differences

286
− 88

288
− 90

364
− 47

367
− 50

Explain your thinking.

Write another set of problems like these.

What Is the Value?

Ramil opened his bank and counted 5 quarters, 16 dimes, 11 nickels, and 56 pennies. What is the total value of his coins?

Tell how you know.

The Answer Is 100

Write at least 5 different addition equations that have this answer.

True or False?

900 is a reasonable estimate for 587 + 394.

900 is a reasonable estimate for 407 + 394.

900 is a reasonable estimate for 587 + 294.

900 is a reasonable estimate for 314 + 497.

Write a more reasonable estimate in at least one of these statements.

Tommy's Tournaments

Tommy organizes all the team tournaments at the Aspen Boys and Girls' Club. He follows these rules when setting up the tournaments.

Rules
- Pair the highest-ranked team against the lowest-ranked team, the second highest-ranked team against the second lowest-ranked team, and so on.
- Make sure there are the correct number of teams in the tournament so that all teams play in each round. No team should get a bye (an advance to the next round without playing).

Here is what a four-team tournament looks like.

Follow Tommy's rules and show tournaments with different numbers of teams. What patterns do you notice? Can you predict how many games would be played in a tournament with 1024 teams? Explain your thinking.

What's an Easy Way?
Computation Review

Solve these problems as quickly as you can. Use the strategies that work best for you.

Find the sum.

1.
```
   52
   27
 +13
 ____
```

2.
```
   74
   32
 +36
 ____
```

3.
```
   55
   45
 +24
 ____
```

4.
```
  348
 +284
 ____
```

5.
```
  934
 +217
 ____
```

6.
```
  759
 +377
 ____
```

Find the next number in each pattern.

7. 1, 4, 7, 10, _____

8. 100, 85, 70, 55, _____

9. 1, 3, 6, 10, 15, _____

10. 4, 8, 12, 16, _____

Solve.

11. $67 + 95$

12. 34×20

13. $73 \div 4$

14. 36×5

15. $154 \div 9$

16. $511 - 32$

17. $68 + 44$

18. $307 - 48$

19. $326 \div 2$

20. $165 \div 8$

▼ **PARENT NOTE:**
To get your child to use his or her own thinking about computations you may ask, *Are there two ways to solve this problem? Is there a way you can do it in your head?*

What's Your Strategy?
Convince Me!

Jimmy and Elise each did the problem 493 − 38 = _____ . Look at their solutions. Notice that Jimmy and Elise got the same, correct answer, but they used different strategies.

Jimmy explained his strategy. The teacher recorded it for the class like this:

Elise used a different strategy. The teacher recorded her explanation like this:

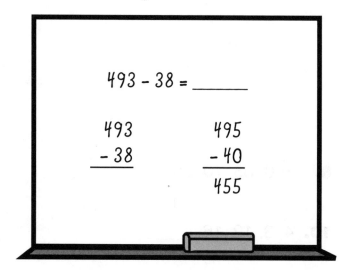

$$493 - 38 = \underline{\hphantom{000}}$$

$$\begin{array}{r} 493 \\ -\ 38 \\ \hline \end{array} \qquad \begin{array}{r} 495 \\ -\ 40 \\ \hline 455 \end{array}$$

$$493 - 38 = \underline{\hphantom{000}}$$

$$493 + 5 = 498$$
$$\underline{-\ 38}$$
$$460 - 5 = 455$$

Solve the problems below. Record your explanation on paper.

1. 371
  − 17

2. 662
  − 29

3. 873
  − 68

4. 584
  − 37

5. 766
  − 58

6. 394
  − 29

▼ PARENT NOTE:
One of the powerful understandings students can gain is that a problem usually has one correct answer but several effective strategies for getting that answer.

Rita's Placemat

Rita designed this placemat using squares of three different colors.

B	R	B	Y	B	R	B
Y	B	R	B	R	B	Y
B	R	B	Y	B	R	B
Y	B	R	B	R	B	Y

Fill in the bubble next to the correct answer.

1. How many yellow squares does she need for one placemat?

○ **A.** 6   ○ **C.** 9

○ **B.** 7   ○ **D.** 28

2. How many blue squares will she need to make 7 placemats?

○ **A.** 14   ○ **C.** 56

○ **B.** 21   ○ **D.** 98

3. Rita has an envelope that contains 3 yellow squares, 2 blue squares and 5 red squares. What fraction of the squares are yellow?

○ **A.** $\frac{1}{10}$ ○ **C.** $\frac{1}{4}$

○ **B.** $\frac{3}{10}$ ○ **D.** $\frac{2}{3}$

4. Rita made 7 placemats Monday, 8 placemats Tuesday and 6 placemats Wednesday. How many did she make in all?

○ **A.** 15   ○ **C.** 22

○ **B.** 21   ○ **D.** 56

5. If the pattern is continued to make a fifth row of the placemat, what would be the order of the squares from left to right?

○ **A.** Blue, red, blue, red, yellow, blue, red

○ **B.** Yellow, blue, red, blue, red, blue, yellow

○ **C.** Blue, red, blue, yellow, blue, red, blue

○ **D.** Yellow, blue, red, yellow, blue, red, yellow

Around Town

On this map, the streets are shown by the grid lines. Each grid unit, ☐ , represents one street block that is 100 meters long. You can go from one place to another only along the streets.

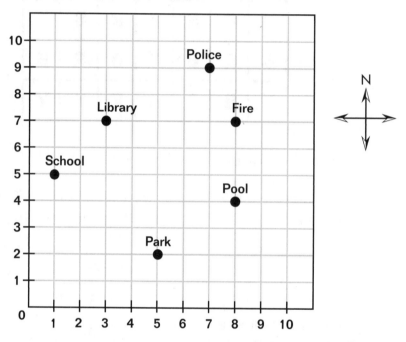

1. The coordinates of the library are (3, 7). What are the coordinates of the community pool?

2. How many meters is it from the school to the park along the shortest street route?

3. List the other 5 places on the map in order according to how far each is from the library. List the closest place first.

4. On Saturday, Jeremy wants to get a book from the library, sign up for swim team at the pool and meet his friends at the park. Describe the different orders he could go to all three places.

5. Which place is west of the pool, south of the police station, and north of the school?

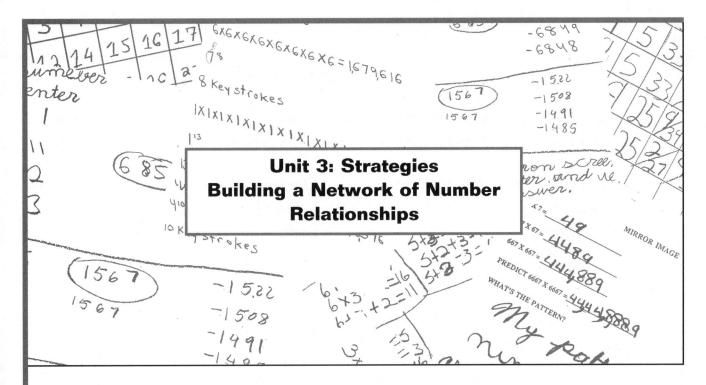

Unit 3: Strategies
Building a Network of Number Relationships

Thinking Questions

What strategies can you use to remember number facts? How can you use finger multiplication to learn the nines facts? What is lattice multiplication? Is there more than one strategy that will help you solve division problems?

Investigations

In this MathLand unit, you will discover answers to these questions and more as your class learns about number relationships. You will learn different ways to solve multiplication and division problems and play games that will help you memorize your fact equations. You will also create your own strategies for solving arithmetic problems and share them with your classmates.

Real-World Math

Using strategies for problem solving is part of what we do every day. It is also important to be able to explain a strategy to someone else who may need to use it. Computer programmers write manuals that explain the strategies they use to design computer programs. The manuals use flowcharts to help other people visualize how these strategies work. How can you be sure that a strategy will work?

Math Vocabulary

During this MathLand unit, you may be using some of these words as you talk and write about strategies for solving math problems.

An **algorithm** is a step-by-step method for solving arithmetic computations.

Example: Multiply 26 × 6.

One algorithm might be:
20 × 6 = 120; 6 × 6 = 36;
120 + 36 = 156.

Another algorithm is:
26 + 26 = 52
26 + 26 = 52 ⟶ 156
26 + 26 = 52

Basic facts are all the combinations you get when you add, subtract, multiply, or divide numbers 0–9.

Example: 5 + 8 = 13, 4 × 8 = 32, 9 − 5 = 4, and 49 ÷ 7 = 7 are all basic facts.

Base ten is a number system that has 10 numerals, 0 through 9. Our number system is a decimal or base ten system.

Decimal numbers are used to show values between any two numbers. Each digit represents a power of 10. Decimal numbers contain a decimal point.

Example: Some of the numbers between 1.2 and 1.3 are: 1.21, 1.22, 1.23, 1.24, 1.25, 1.26, 1.27, 1.28, and 1.29.

A **digit** is any one of the ten number symbols, 0 through 9.

A **strategy** is a plan for solving a problem.

Example: Using a pattern to make a prediction is a strategy.

Crossword Strategies

Use the clues and the words in the word puzzle.

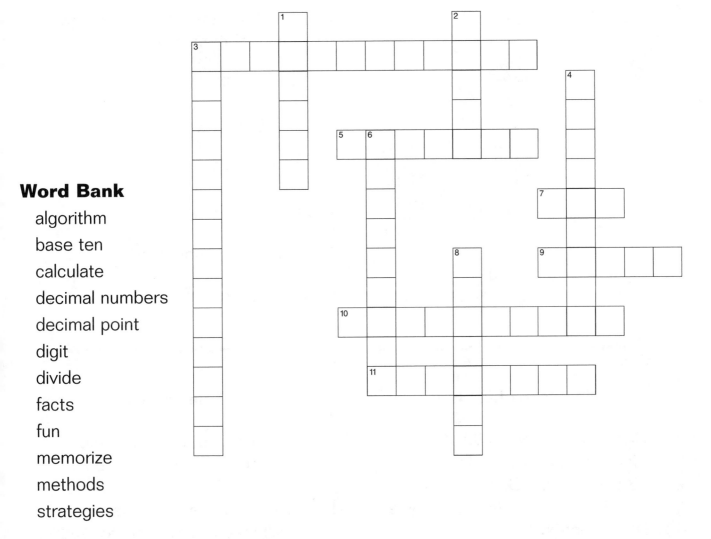

Word Bank

algorithm

base ten

calculate

decimal numbers

decimal point

digit

divide

facts

fun

memorize

methods

strategies

Across

3. Decimal numbers contain a _____ _____.

5. Our number system

7. Math is _____!

9. Students learn arithmetic _____.

10. _____ are plans for solving problems.

11. to learn by heart

Down

1. to separate into equal groups

2. 3

3. numbers between numbers

4. to do a math process

6. a step-by-step procedure

8. ways of doing something

1

Solve

$12 \times 7 =$ _____

Tell how you know.

2

Choose the Correct Answer

4×9 has the same answer as which of the following?

A 7×5

B 6×7

C 2×16

D 3×12

Explain how you know.

3

What Is the Best Buy?

Can A of juice costs $0.48 for 12 ounces, Can B costs $0.89 for 18 ounces, and Can C costs $1.69 for 36 ounces. Which juice is the best buy?

Explain how you know.

4

True or False?

Suppose you read the same number of pages in your book each day. True or false? If you read 64 pages in 8 days, then it will take you 16 days to read 128 pages.

Explain your thinking.

PARENT NOTE:
Discuss problems like number 3 and explain how you figure out the best buy for your family. In this way, your child can see that math is useful in everyday life.

1

Find the Quotient

$84 \div 2 =$ _____

Tell how you know.

2

Choose the Best Answer

19×6 is closest to:

A   100

B   125

C   150

D   175

Explain your thinking.

3

How Many Ride Bikes to School?

There are 30 students in Mrs. Chase's class. One fifth of them ride their bikes to school. How many students ride their bikes to school? How many students do not ride their bikes to school?

Show your thinking.

4

True or False?

If movie tickets cost $3.25 each, then 5 tickets cost $15.75.

Explain your answer.

PARENT NOTE:
When students have strong number sense, they are able to solve problems like number 1 in a variety of ways. Ask your child to explain how he or she solved this problem.

Name _____

Write the Answers

56 × 2 = _____

28 × 4 = _____

14 × 8 = _____

7 × 16 = _____

Show your thinking.

Choose the Correct Answer

Jessica's family went on a trip. On Monday they drove 389 miles. On Tuesday they drove 294 miles. How much farther did they travel on Monday than on Tuesday?

A   195 miles   C   85 miles

B   105 miles   D   95 miles

Tell how you know.

The Answer Is 18

Find 2 sets of numbers that have an average of 18.

Field Trip

There are 465 students at Forest Glen School. All the students are going by bus to the museum. Each bus holds 85 people. How many buses do they need for their trip? If 31 adults go along, will there be enough room for them on the same number of buses?

Explain your thinking.

Hidden Facts

There are 15 multiplication facts hidden in this puzzle. One is shown. The facts may be written in a row, in a column, or on a diagonal. Can you find the other 14 facts?

64	35	64	20	5	4	27	32
9	8	70	6	42	7	4	26
8	4	3	12	4	8	9	16
32	15	5	24	8	56	35	63
9	25	7	6	42	4	8	35
5	4	35	3	6	4	30	3
54	3	36	24	54	6	9	5
8	5	9	45	6	4	5	15

What's a Good Estimate?
Greater Than, Less Than

Build your estimation skills. For each problem, tell if the answer will be less than (<) or greater than (>) the estimate given. Explain why you think so.

1. 24 x 42   is _____ than 800 because _____

_____

2. 653 ÷ 8   is _____ than 80 because _____

_____

3. $\frac{1}{2}$ of 5   is _____ than 3 because _____

_____

4. 715 ÷ 8   is _____ than 90 because _____

_____

5. 49 x 12   is _____ than 600 because _____

_____

Now, write a problem like one on this page.

▼ **PARENT NOTE:**
By pointing out situations in which you use estimation, you can help your child appreciate these real-life skills. Let your child help you with an estimation whenever you have a chance.

1

Find the Sum

282
+ 459

Explain your thinking.

2

Choose the Correct Answer

Which equation is false?

A $150 \div 10 = 15$

B $1200 \div 4 = 30$

C $3000 \div 6 = 500$

D $350 \div 7 = 50$

Tell how you know.

3

Fences

Raul is building a pentagon-shaped pen for his lambs. Three sides of the pen are each 13 ft long; the other two sides are each 11 ft long. How many feet of fence does Raul need to buy?

Explain how you know.

4

Which Is Greater?

Put < or > in each circle to show which is greater.

$62 - $23.68 ◯ $62 - $24.68

$62 - $23.68 ◯ $61 - $23.68

$62 - $23.68 ◯ $62 - $22.68

Explain how you know.

Divide

8)‾896‾

Show your thinking.

Choose the Closest Estimate

38 + 21 + 17 + 68

A   More than 100

B   Between 125 and 150

C   Between 150 and 175

D   More than 175

Explain your thinking.

How Much Change Do You Get?

At the book store you buy
4 paperback books that cost
$0.95 each. You give the clerk
$10.00. How much change will
you get?

Explain how you know.

True or False?

240 s = 40 min

120 s = 20 min

2400 s = 40 min

If any statements are false,
change them to true ones.

1

Find the Product

$14 \times 16 =$ _____

Show your thinking.

2

Choose the Correct Answer

The builder needs to put a fence around the new swimming pool. The area is a rectangle that is 52 yd by 43 yd. How many feet of fencing does the builder need?

A   2184 ft   C   570 ft

B   190 ft   D   285 ft

Explain how you know.

3

The Answer Is 30

Write at least 4 multiplication equations that have this answer.

4

Agree or Disagree?

Sandra said that $472 \div 6$ is less than 75. Do you agree or disagree?

Tell how you know.

Agree or Disagree?

The teacher gave Duyen this problem:

The answer is 36. Write at least 6 equations that have this answer.

Do you agree or disagree with Duyen's work?
Explain your thinking.

There are lots of ways to make 36 by
using + − x ÷

These are some equations of 36
There are many more but some
of these are easier.

1. $(30 + 6 = 36)$
2. $(31 + 5 = 36)$
3. $(10 + 26 = 36)$
4. $(36 ÷ 1 = 36)$
5. $(108 ÷ 3 = 36)$
6. $(6 × 6 = 36)$
7. $(9 × 4 = 36)$
8. $(40 − 4 = 36)$
9. $(38 − 2 = 36)$
10. $(29 + 7 = 36)$
11. $(6 × 2 × 3 = 36)$
12. $(30 + 10 − 4 = 36)$
13. $(8 + 18 = 36)$
14. $(7 + 19 = 36)$
15. $(50 − 30 + 16 = 36)$
16. $(60 − 30 + 6 = 36)$
17. $(2 × 6 + 14 = 36)$
18. $(5 + 5 + 5 + 5 + 5 + 5 + 1 = 36)$
19. $(1 + 35 = 36)$
20. $(10 × 2 + 16 = 36)$
21. $(72 ÷ 2 = 36)$
22. $(66 − 30 = 36)$
23. $(65 − 31 = 36)$
24. $(36 + 0 = 36)$

▼ PARENT NOTE:

On a page like this, students see that there is more than one way to write the same number. By looking at another student's work, they see possibilities they may not have considered themselves. They also strengthen their computation skills as they check for any incorrect responses.

What's an Easy Way?
Computation Review

Solve these problems as quickly as you can. Use the strategies that work best for you.

Multiply.

1.	32 × 7	**2.**	78 × 3	**3.**	102 × 9

4.	34 × 12	**5.**	56 × 15	**6.**	623 × 14

Divide.

7. $5\overline{)565}$ **8.** $7\overline{)847}$ **9.** $4\overline{)391}$

10. $6\overline{)324}$ **11.** $3\overline{)107}$ **12.** $8\overline{)914}$

Solve.

13.	26 × 4	**14.**	321 +186	**15.**	622 − 358

16. $6\overline{)738}$

17. 89
× 5

18. 92
49
+ 27

19. 425
× 8
3400

20. $4\overline{)222}$

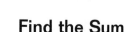

1

Find the Sum

672
+ 398

Explain how you know.

2

Choose the Correct Answer

Which has the same answer as
239 + 148 = _____ ?

A   179 + 218 = _____

B   348 + 49 = _____

C   112 + 265 = _____

D   228 + 159 = _____

Show your thinking.

3

Is $10.00 Enough?

Steve went to the post office to buy 32¢ stamps. He had $10.00. Did he have enough money to buy 30 stamps?

Tell how you know.

4

Agree or Disagree?

Dawn said that if you travel 30 mi in 1 hr, you will go the same speed as you would if you travel 15 mi in 30 min. Do you agree or disagree?

Explain your answer.

1

Find the Differences

```
  178        179
-  49      -  50


  235        237
-  18      -  20
```

Explain your thinking.

2

Choose the Correct Answer

Kelly arrived at the soccer field at 4:25 P.M. Jesse arrived at the field 1 hr 35 min before Kelly. What time did Jesse arrive?

A   2:50 P.M.

B   3:05 P.M.

C   5:55 P.M.

D   2:55 P.M.

Tell how you know.

3

Solve

Kathryn invited 8 friends over for pizza. Each person ate $\frac{1}{3}$ of a pizza. How many pizzas did Kathryn need?

Explain your thinking.

4

Agree or Disagree?

Travis has 145 nickels in his bank. He said the value of the nickels is $7.25. Do you agree or disagree?

Explain your answer.

PARENT NOTE:
Problems like number 1 help students to develop new strategies that can help in mental computation.
Ask your child to make up another problem that could be solved using the same strategy.

Divide

$3.75 \div \$0.25 = \underline{\hspace{1cm}}$

Show your work.

Choose the Correct Answer

Which has an answer of 948?

A   387 + 661 = \underline{\hspace{1cm}}

B   1087 − 149 = \underline{\hspace{1cm}}

C   729 + 229 = \underline{\hspace{1cm}}

D   1284 − 336 = \underline{\hspace{1cm}}

Tell how you know.

The Answer Is 5

Write 8 division equations that have this answer.

Solve

Tracy walked 1.2 mi from school to home. She then walked 0.7 mi to her friend's house. They walked 0.5 mi to the park. Tracy walked the same way, back to her friend's house and then home. How far did she walk all together?

Explain your thinking.

What Did They Eat?

Rashad, Calvin, Sonia, Elisa, and Madison went to the movies together. They each had $15.00. They each bought a ticket and a snack. No one bought the same snack as anyone else. What snack did each person buy?

Movie Tickets: $7.00

Popcorn		**Soda**		**Candy**	
Large	$3.75	Large	$2.75	Mints	$1.75
Medium	$3.00	Medium	$2.00	Fruit Disks	$1.25
Small	$2.25	Small	$1.50	Chocolate Bar	$2.50

Amount of Change

Rashad	$2.25	Sonia	$6.75	Madison	$5.50
Calvin	$0.50	Elisa	$4.25		

---

1. Rashad _____

2. Calvin _____

3. Sonia _____

4. Elisa _____

5. Madison _____

▼ PARENT NOTE:
Pages like this help students build strong problem-solving skills. There are many strategies students might use to find the correct solution.

What's Your Strategy?
Convince Me!

Mike and Shemika solved the problem $46 \times 8 =$ _____. Look at their solutions. Notice that Mike and Shemika got the same, correct answer, but they used different strategies.

Mike explained his strategy.
The teacher recorded it for the class like this:

Shemika explained her strategy.
The teacher recorded it for the class like this:

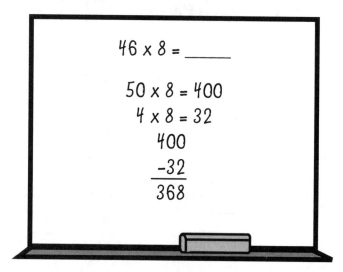

Mike:

$46 \times 8 =$ _____

$50 \times 8 = 400$
$4 \times 8 = 32$
400
$\underline{-32}$
368

Shemika:

$46 \times 8 =$ _____

$40 \times 8 = 320$
$6 \times 8 = \underline{48}$
368

Solve the problems below. Record your explanation on paper.

1. $24 \times 4 =$ _____

2. $64 \times 8 =$ _____

3. $320 \times 4 =$ _____

4. $524 \times 6 =$ _____

5. $432 \times 2 =$ _____

6. $280 \times 8 =$ _____

Find the Product

26
× 11

Explain your thinking.

Which Answer Is Correct?

(24 ÷ 3) × 2 = _____

A   12

B   16

C   8

D   4

Show your thinking.

What Is the Average?

Heather recorded the amount of time she spent on homework for the week: Monday, 55 min; Tuesday, 39 min; Wednesday, 70 min; Thursday, 46 min; and Friday, 0 min. What was the average daily time Heather spent on homework for the week?

Explain your thinking.

Agree or Disagree?

Tuan used his calculator to compute 400 ÷ 20. He got an answer of 200. Tuan thought the answer was a reasonable one. Do you agree or disagree?

Tell how you know.

Find the Quotient

$$74\overline{)178}$$

Show your thinking.

Choose the Correct Answer

Grace rides the bus every day. Her fares for one week were: Monday, $1.05; Tuesday, $2.10; Wednesday, $0.75; Thursday, $2.10; Friday, $1.05. How much did the bus cost for the week?

A $7.05   C $7.50

B $6.05   D $7.95

Tell how you know.

Solve

There are 80 members in the Center Avenue School band. Fourteen players sit in each row of chairs. How many rows of chairs are there? If 5 more people join the band, will they need another row of chairs?

Explain your thinking.

True or False?

893 ÷ 21 is about 45.

719 ÷ 82 is about 90.

493 ÷ 12 is about 40.

Can you write a more reasonable estimate for any of these?

PARENT NOTE:
Pay close attention to your child's thinking about a problem, not just the answer. Learning how to approach problems is a valuable life-long skill.

Find the Answer

$\frac{3}{8}$ of 16 = _____

Explain your thinking.

Choose the Closest Estimate

Gary bought 3 shirts for $8.98 each and 2 pairs of jeans for $15.89 each. He paid $3.53 tax. About how much did he spend?

A $55

B $60

C $65

D $70

Tell how you know.

The Answer Is 47

Write at least 6 addition equations that have this answer.

True or False?

These equations have the same answer.

(Hint: Solve inside the parentheses first.)

$(11-8)+(3+6)+(12-8)=$ _____

$11-(8+3)+(6+12)-8=$ _____

What can you say about adding and subtracting a series of numbers?

Calculator Calculations

What keys did Billy press on his calculator to get from one number to the next? Find two different ways for each set of numbers.

1.

24

÷2   −12

12

6

1

5

15

2.

5

25

50

100

5

30

3.

5

40

80

5

45

9

4.

100

50

10

20

5

100

5.

21

3

18

36

6

18

6.

4

2

1

24

4

28

What's a Good Estimate?
It's Between ...

Build your estimation skills. For each problem, write two numbers, one number that is greater than and one number that is less than the exact answer would be. Then explain why you chose those numbers.

$$726 \\ + \ 202$$

_____ and _____

Why? _____

_____

$$86 \\ \times \ 7$$

_____ and _____

Why? _____

_____

$612 - 389 = $ _____

_____ and _____

Why? _____

_____

$93 \div 7 = $ _____

_____ and _____

Why? _____

_____

Gloria's class is selling decorated notepads to raise money for the rainforest. They decorated 48 notebooks and will sell them for $1.25 each. How much will they earn if they sell all the notebooks?

The amount they will collect is between $ _____ and $ _____ .

Why? _____

Name _____

Find the Sums

27	32
35	29
49	48
+11	+51

63	81
76	24
27	23
+34	+46

Explain your thinking.

Choose the Correct Answer

25 × 17 = _____

A   525

B   42

C   425

D   475

Tell how you know.

What Is the Daily Cost?

Noah's dad rides rapid transit to work 5 days a week. He buys an 8-week pass for $85. A 1-day pass costs $2.45. Which is the better deal?

Explain your thinking.

True or False?

50 × 30 > 1200

55 × 25 > 1200

60 × 20 > 1200

If any statements are false, write one way to make them true.

PARENT NOTE:
In problem number 1, a useful strategy is looking for pairs of numbers that have a sum of 10. This program provides many opportunities for students to learn and practice mental computation in a variety of ways.

1
Find the Product

76 × 4 = _____

Show your work.

2
Choose the Correct Answer

Karin helps her aunt at the gift shop. She works from 10:15 A.M. until 2:40 P.M. How long does she work?

A   5 hr 25 min

B   4 hr 25 min

C   4 hr 30 min

D   5 hr 30 min

Explain your thinking.

3
What Are the Ages?

Violeta is 3 years older than her brother. Both of their ages together equal 21 years. How old is Violeta? How old is her brother?

Tell how you know.

4
How Much More?

A plane ticket to Dallas costs $342. A ticket to Seattle costs $178.50. How much more does it cost to fly to Dallas?

Show your work.

Name _____

1

Divide

$25 \overline{)150}$

$25 \overline{)155}$

$25 \overline{)250}$

Which problem did you solve first? Did you use that solution to solve the others? If so, how?

2

Find the Missing Factor

$24 \times \underline{\hspace{1cm}} = 384$

A   24

B   16

C   18

D   21

Tell how you know.

3

The Answer Is 48

Write at least 6 multiplication equations that have this answer.

4

Rhea's Report

Rhea worked hard on her social studies report. The different amounts of time she worked were: 45 min, 20 min, 55 min, 1 hr 10 min, 35 min. How much time did she spend all together on her report?

Explain your thinking.

Magic Squares

Which are "magic" squares? Multiply the numbers in each row, each column, and along each diagonal. If a square has the same product in each direction, it is "magic."

1.

4	100	10
50	20	8
40	2	100

2.

48	9	4
1	12	144
36	16	3

3.

2	25	20
100	10	1
5	4	50

4.

4	60	2
4	8	15
30	1	16

What's an Easy Way?
Computation Review

Solve these problems as quickly as you can. Use the strategies that work best for you.

Divide.

1. $21 \overline{)439}$ **2.** $48 \overline{)623}$ **3.** $22 \overline{)398}$

4. $12 \overline{)313}$ **5.** $37 \overline{)562}$ **6.** $21 \overline{)476}$

Multiply.

7. 15×20 **8.** 63×60 **9.** 34×80

10. 26×30 **11.** 74×40 **12.** 52×50

Solve.

13. $826 + 43$ **14.** $472 - 48$ **15.** 39×6

16. $\frac{1}{7}$ of 35 **17.** $\frac{1}{4}$ of 12 **18.** $\frac{1}{5}$ of 45

19. 91×8 **20.** $341 \div 3$

Name _____

Sunrise and Sunset

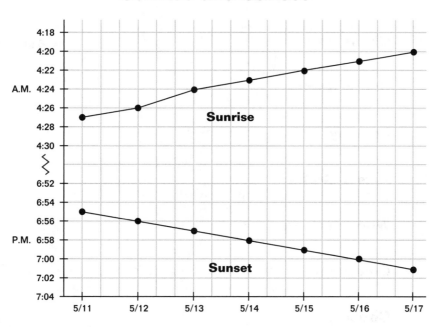

Use information from the graph to answer these questions.
Fill in the bubble next to the correct answer.

1. Which day had the most amount of daylight?

   ○ **A.** May 1   ○ **C.** May 15

   ○ **B.** May 11   ○ **D.** May 17

2. When did the sun rise on May 13?

   ○ **A.** 4:26 A.M.   ○ **C.** 6:56 P.M.

   ○ **B.** 4:24 A.M.   ○ **D.** 6:57 P.M.

3. How many hours and minutes of daylight were there on May 14?

   ○ **A.** 2 hours 33 minutes

   ○ **B.** 12 hours 33 minutes

   ○ **C.** 14 hours 35 minutes

   ○ **D.** none of the above

4. How many minutes later did the sun set on May 15 than on May 12?

   ○ **A.** 2 minutes   ○ **C.** 6 minutes

   ○ **B.** 3 minutes   ○ **D.** 8 minutes

5. Which is the best estimate of the time of sunrise on May 29th?

   ○ **A.** 4:08 A.M.   ○ **C.** 4:14 A.M.

   ○ **B.** 4:12 A.M.   ○ **D.** 4:32 A.M.

Student Activity Clubs

Chess

Board Games

Ecology

Arts & Crafts

Woodworking

Computer

Cooking

$\overset{\circ}{\underset{\wedge}{\uparrow}}$ = 4 students

Use the pictograph to answer the following questions.

1. Each member of the ecology club donated $1.50 for printing a recycling information book. How much did they donate in all?

2. Three people belong to both the cooking and arts and crafts clubs. How many students belong to either of these two clubs?

3. Each member of the computer club is allowed 20 minutes on line each month. What is the most hours and minutes the club could use in one month?

4. One-fourth of the members of the woodworking club do some woodworking at home. How many members is this?

5. A fabric shop donated 20 yards of fabric to the arts and crafts club. How many feet of fabric would each member get if it is divided evenly?

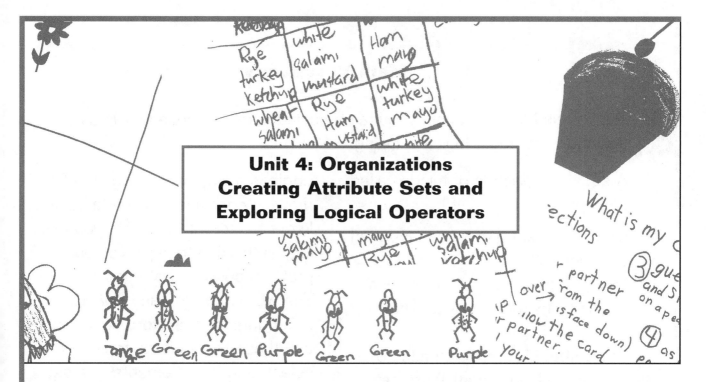

Thinking Questions

How many different houses can you create using a flat or sloped roof, three or four windows, one or two stories, and a brick, stone, or cement walkway? What is the relationship between the number of possible combinations and the number of choices for each category? What is a Venn diagram and how is it used?

Investigations

In this MathLand unit, you will learn how to identify the attributes and options for a set of objects, and you will learn how to describe and organize the possible combinations of objects. You will also create diagrams to demonstrate different organizations of objects.

Real-World Math

Logical thinking is important in games we play and work that we do every day. Watch for ways that people use logical thinking in decision making at home or at school. How can you be sure that you have included all the possible choices in a problem about combinations?

Math Vocabulary

During this MathLand unit, you may be using some of these words as you talk and write about logical thinking.

A **set** is a collection of things called **elements**.

Example: A set that names types of transportation might have cars, bicycles, trains, skateboards, and hot air balloons as its elements.

An **attribute** is a characteristic of a person or thing. An **attribute set** shows all the different combinations you can make with a certain set of characteristics, such as size, shape, or color.

Example: At the store, you see yellow, red, and green apples. Some of the apples are small and some are large. What is the attribute set of all the different apples you can buy today?

Logic is a way of thinking about and drawing conclusions from facts you know are true. In this unit, you use logical thinking to improve your problem-solving strategies. The words *and*, *or*, and *not* are called **logical operators**. You can use these three words to compare, select, and sort elements of a set.

A **category** is a system of classification. A category can be very broad or narrow.

Example: The category of "houses" can contain hundreds of different types of houses for humans and animals.

small red apple   small yellow apple   small green apple

large red apple   large yellow apple   large green apple

Categories

Find each word from the word bank in the block of letters.
Words may go in any direction. Longer words may wrap around two rows or columns.

Word Bank

and
attribute
attribute sets
categories
logical operators
logic
not
or
select
set
shape
size

L	S	E	I	R	O	G	E	T	A	C
O	S	E	T	U	B	I	R	T	T	A
G	E	S	E	L	E	C	T	R	O	L
I	T	A	N	D	T	O	N	S	M	O
C	S	H	A	P	E	S	I	Z	E	G
A	A	T	T	R	I	B	U	T	E	I
L	O	P	E	R	A	T	O	R	S	C

Use the words from the word bank to answer the questions.

1. ___ __ __ __ __ __ __ __   __ __ __ __ __ __ __ __ __ __ are the words ___ ___ ___, ___ ___ ___, and ___ ___ that allow us to compare, ___ ___ ___ ___ ___ ___, and sort elements of a set.

2. ___ __ __ __ __ __ __ __ __ __   __ __ __ __ show all the different combinations you can make with a certain ___ ___ ___ of characteristics, such as ___ ___ ___ ___, ___ ___ ___ ___ ___, or color.

3. ___ __ __ __ __ __ __ __ __ __ may be used in classification.

4. ___ ___ ___ ___ ___ is a way to think about facts you know are true.

5. A characteristic of a person or thing is an ___ ___ ___ ___ ___ ___ ___ ___ ___ .

▼ PARENT NOTE:
Make a list with your child of all the attributes you can think of that describe a favorite toy or pet.

Name _____

Find the Answer

12 × 19 = _____

Explain your thinking.

Choose the Correct Answer

Daniel shared his 149 peanuts equally with 2 friends. How did he divide the peanuts so everyone got a fair share?

A   48 peanuts each, 1 left over

B   49 peanuts each

C   49 peanuts each, 2 left over

D   48 peanuts each

Tell how you know.

Agree or Disagree?

Ann said you can make 24 different ice cream sundaes if you have 4 flavors of ice cream, 3 different toppings, and a choice of using whipped cream or not. Do you agree or disagree? (Each sundae has 1 kind of ice cream, 1 topping, and whipped cream or no whipped cream.)

Tell how you know.

True or False?

Celia's scout group raised money to go to camp. All together they have $592.34. There are 7 girls in the group. True or false? Each girl will get $88.55 for camp.

Show your thinking.

Name _____

Subtract

823 −276	827 −280
645 −397	648 −400

Explain your thinking.

Write another set of problems like these.

Choose the Correct Answer

Clarissa turned 11 years old in March. How many months old is she in August?

A   126 months

B   172 months

C   136 months

D   137 months

Show your thinking.

Solve

The players on Anthony's soccer team are either 10 or 11 years old. There are 21 players in all. There are 5 more 11-year-olds than 10-year-olds. How many players are 11 years old? How many are 10 years old?

Tell how you know.

True or False?

$(16 \times 2) + (25 \times 3) − 55 = 47$

$16 + (2 \times 25) + 3 − 55 = 14$

$(16 \times 2) + (25 \times 3) − 60 = 47$

If any statements are false, change them to true ones.

▼ **PARENT NOTE:**

One of the most powerful understandings students can gain is that a problem usually has one correct answer, but several effective strategies for finding the answer.

Name _____

 1

Find the Sum

683 + 498 = _____

Show your thinking.

 2

Which Is the Best Answer?

9438 − 6189 = _____

A   About 320

B   Exactly 3259

C   About 3200

D   Exactly 3159

Explain your work.

 3

The Answer Is 10

Show at least 5 division equations that have this answer.

 4

True or False?

During the week Michelle's mom spent $28.90 for lunches. True or false? She spent an average of $5.78 on each of the 5 days.

Tell how you know.

Wrap It Up!

Mattie Moore took her mom's birthday present to Gerald's Gift Wrapping Service to be wrapped. She had the following choices.

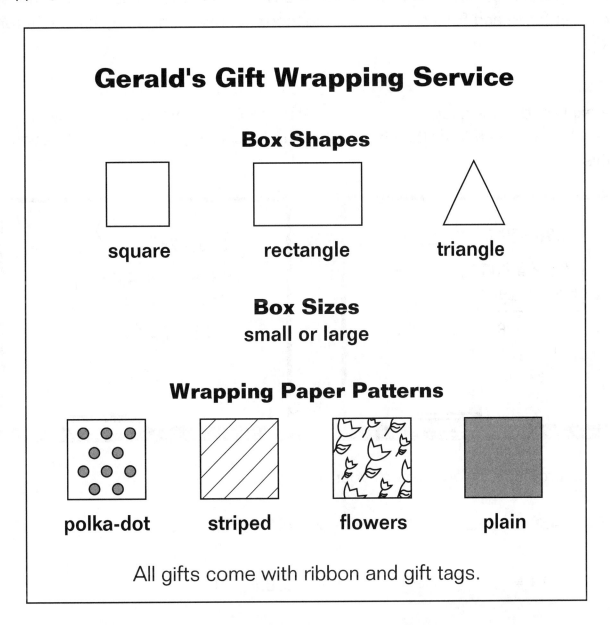

Show all the different ways that Mattie Moore could get her present wrapped. How many ways are there? Tell how you know you have shown them all.

▼ **PARENT NOTE:**
To solve the problem presented here, students must have an organized method of listing all the possible choices. Ask your child to explain his or her method.

What's Your Strategy?
Convince Me!

Elena and Robert solved the problem 396 + 247 = _____. Look at their solutions. Notice that Elena and Robert got the same, correct answer, but they used different strategies.

Elena explained her strategy.
The teacher recorded it for the class like this:

Robert used a different strategy.
The teacher recorded his explanation like this:

$$396 + 247 = \underline{\quad}$$
$$396 + 4 = 400$$
$$+\ 247 \qquad +247$$
$$\overline{}$$
$$647 - 4 = 643$$

$$396 + 247 = \underline{\quad}$$
$$396 + 200 = 596$$
$$596 + 40 = 636$$
$$636 + 7 = 643$$

Solve the problems below. Record your explanation on paper.

1. 293 + 468 = _____

2. 790 + 172 = _____

3. 495 + 273 = _____

4. 596 + 321 = _____

5. 691 + 342 = _____

6. 394 + 458 = _____

▼ **PARENT NOTE:**
A good strategy for solving one problem may not be as good for another problem. Students who are able to handle numbers in many ways think about the particular numbers in a problem to decide what strategy they will use.

1

Find the Products

$64 \times 15 =$ _____

$32 \times 30 =$ _____

$78 \times 25 =$ _____

$39 \times 50 =$ _____

Tell how you know.

Write another set of problems like these.

2

Choose the Correct Answer

Julio took $30 to the park. He spent $16.50 for tickets, $2.18 for a hot dog, $0.92 for a drink, and $4.73 for a cap. How much did he have left?

A $0   C $5.67

B $5.77   D $6.27

Explain your thinking.

3

What's Your Story?

Write a story problem for $248 \div 8$. Show your solution.

4

What Are the Possibilities?

Matt has 5 shirts, 3 pairs of pants, and a reversible belt. All the items go together. How many different outfits can Matt wear?

Explain your thinking.

Name _____

Find the Quotient

$$50 \overline{) \$10.50}$$

Explain your answer.

2

What Time Did He Return?

Jacob left home at 3:20. It took him 20 min to ride his bike to swim practice. He practiced for 1 hr. He visited with his friends for 45 min, and then he went home. If it took him the same amount of time to ride home, what time did he arrive home?

Tell how you know.

3

Solve

Lyse spelled 84 words correctly on the Spell-A-Thon. Twelve people pledged 10¢ for each word she spelled correctly, and 6 people pledged 14¢ for each correct word. How much money did Lyse collect all together?

Show your thinking.

4

Which Is Greater?

4712 − 1083 ◯ 3600.

3208 − 982 ◯ 2300.

7546 − 4487 ◯ 3000.

Put < or > in each circle to make a true statement.

1

Find the Difference

469
− 372
‾‾‾‾‾

Explain your work.

2

Choose the Correct Answer

With which 3 numbers can you write a true equation?

A   12, 3, 8

B   36, 3, 118

C   36, 12, 24

D   25, 4, 120

Tell how you know.

3

The Answer Is 15

Write 8 subtraction equations that have this answer.

4

Disks for the Class

Mr. Fujimoto bought 7 boxes of floppy disks for the computer class. Each box holds 12 disks and costs $8.37. How many floppy disks are there all together? If Mr. Fujimoto had $60, did he have enough money?

Show your thinking.

Who Is Who?

1. Which hobby do Latisha, Leroy, Eva, Jack, and Henry each like?

_____   _____   _____   _____   _____

- Leroy and Henry don't know how to draw.
- The basketball player and Henry are friends.
- The skate boarder and Latisha are the same age.
- Henry and the gardener are neighbors.
- The skate boarder is Leroy's sister.
- Latisha doesn't play basketball nor does she garden.
- Jack and the gardener are in the same class.

2. Which footwear do Meg, Ted, Jermaine, Bev, and Andrew each wear?

_____   _____   _____   _____   _____

- Ted doesn't skate or hike.
- Andrew is afraid of the water.
- Bev says that running is bad for her knees.
- Jermaine thinks cowboy boots are uncomfortable.
- The runner is Ted's sister.
- Ted doesn't wear shoes with pointed toes.
- Jermaine and the skater are brothers.

▼ **PARENT NOTE:**
Students use logic to answer these questions. They often find solving these kinds of problems especially rewarding.

What's a Good Estimate?
Greater Than, Less Than

Build your estimation skills. For each problem, tell if the answer will be less than (<) or greater than (>) the estimate given. Explain why you think so.

1. 4.2×5.39 is _____ than 20 because _____

_____

2. $7.9 + 8.3 + 7.5$ is _____ than 21 because _____

_____

3. $60 \overline{)471}$ is _____ than 8 because _____

_____

4. $279 - 82$ is _____ than 200 because _____

_____

5. $65.2 \div 7$ is _____ than 9 because _____

_____

Now, write a problem like one on this page.

What's an Easy Way?
Computation Review

Solve these problems as quickly as you can. Use the strategies that work best for you.

Multiply.

1. 63×40

2. 78×40

3. 49×600

4. 42×30

5. 675×20

6. 831×5

Divide.

7. $3 \overline{)501}$

8. $4 \overline{)236}$

9. $8 \overline{)312}$

10. $6 \overline{)426}$

11. $5 \overline{)6585}$

12. $2 \overline{)132}$

Solve.

13. $65 + 27$

14. $981 - 28$

15. 54×16

16. $456 \div 12$

17. $8.23 + 2.6$

18. $4.3 - 1.7$

19. $395 + 312$

20. $871 - 278$

Fred's Diner

This graph shows the number of people in Fred's Diner at certain times of the day.

Fill in the bubble next to the correct answer.

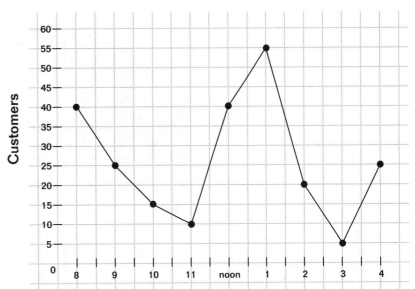

1. How many more people were in the diner at noon than at 10:00 am?

○ **A.** 15   ○ **C.** 40

○ **B.** 25   ○ **D.** 65

2. Which statement is true?

○ **A.** There were 25 fewer people in the diner at 1:00 pm than at noon.

○ **B.** There were 20 more people in the diner at 4:00 pm than at 3:00.

○ **C.** There were 15 more people in the diner at 9:00 am than at 8:00 am.

○ **D.** There were 25 fewer people in the diner at 2:00 pm than at 1:00 pm.

3. A customer paid her check for $4.50 and her friend's check for $3.75. She gave the cashier $20.00. How much change should she get?

○ **A.** $2.75   ○ **C.** $11.75

○ **B.** $8.25   ○ **D.** $12.25

4. Fred offers turkey, ham, tuna, and cheese sandwiches every day. Each sandwich can be made on white, wheat, or rye bread. Sandwiches can have mayonnaise or mustard, none or both. How many different sandwich combinations can Fred make based on these choices?

○ **A.** 11   ○ **C.** 24

○ **B.** 12   ○ **D.** 48

5. A customer spilled some food on his check and can't read part of it. What must the missing digit be?

○ **A.** 7   ○ **C.** 70

○ **B.** 8   ○ **D.** 80

Diner Check

H. Sand.	4.?5
Tea	.75
Pie	1.35
	$6.85

thank you!

Fun With a Spinner

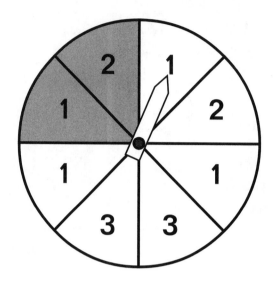

1. What fraction of the spinner is shaded?

2. If you spin the spinner 100 times, what number will you get most of the time?

3. What is the probability that the spinner will land on 2 if it is spun one time?

4. Marci and Ellen are using the spinner to move pieces on a board game. Marci has 11 spaces to go before she reaches the goal. What is the least possible number of turns she needs to win?

5. Three friends are using the spinner to play a game. This chart shows the results:

Name	Number on Spin
Leroy	1, 1, 3, 2, 1
Ben	2, 2, 1, 1, 3
Frank	1, 2, 1, 1, 1

The winner is the player with the highest total after 6 spins. Leroy spins 1 on the next turn. What is the least number Ben needs to be sure to win? Can Frank win?

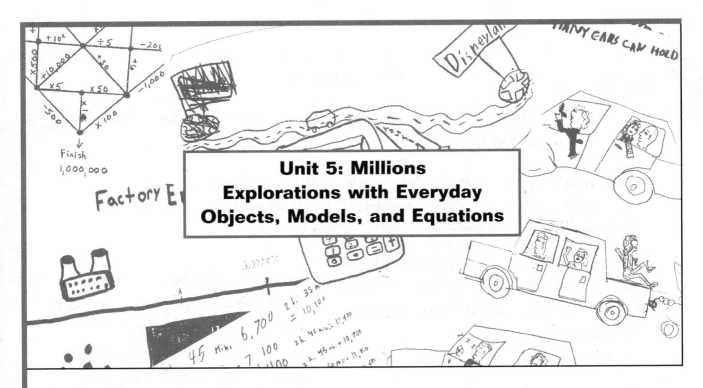

Thinking Questions

How long would it take to count to one million? How could you make a model of a millions block? What are some different ways to describe one million? How many 1000s are in 1,000,000? What else can you say about a million?

Investigations

In this MathLand unit, you will discover answers to these questions and more as your class explores millions using everyday objects, models, and equations. You will learn how to use estimation to count to one million, and you will explore different ways to name a million. You will also learn how to create a number line to visualize relationships among large numbers.

Real-World Math

Notice how large numbers are used in the newspaper every day to inform us about events in the worlds of science, business, and sports. What are some ways in which you could use large numbers in your favorite sport or hobby?

Math Vocabulary

During this MathLand unit, you may be using some of these words as you talk and write about large numbers.

A **benchmark** is a point of reference. In this unit, you will be working with millions.

Example: You may not be able to weigh a million pennies, but you can weigh 100 pennies and use this as a benchmark to understand how much more a million pennies would weigh.

An **equation** is a number sentence. It includes equal values on both sides of an equal sign.

Example: $10 \times 11 = 110$

An **estimate** is an approximate amount. It is based on some experience and calculation.

Example: By counting the number of bleachers and the people in 1 row of bleachers, Matt estimated there were about 500 people at the game.

An **exponent** is a small number written above and to the right of another number called the **base**. The exponent indicates how many times to multiply the base by itself.

Example: $5^4 = 5 \times 5 \times 5 \times 5$

base   exponent

Place value is the value of a digit based on where the digit is in a numeral.

Decimal numbers are used to show values between any two numbers. They contain a decimal point. Decimal numbers can be greater than 1, such as 2.5, 4.674, or 1.11111. Decimal numbers can be less than 1, such as 0.5555, 0.6, 0.999999999.

Place Value Chart	millions	hundred thousands	ten thousands	thousands	hundreds	tens	ones	decimal point	tenths	hundredths	thousandths
1,023,006.203	1	0	2	3	0	0	6	.	2	0	3
669,408.36		6	6	9	4	0	8	.	3	6	

Name _____

Millions of Stars

Color all decimal numbers black.
Color all numbers with exponents red.
Color each correct equation orange.
Color each estimate yellow.

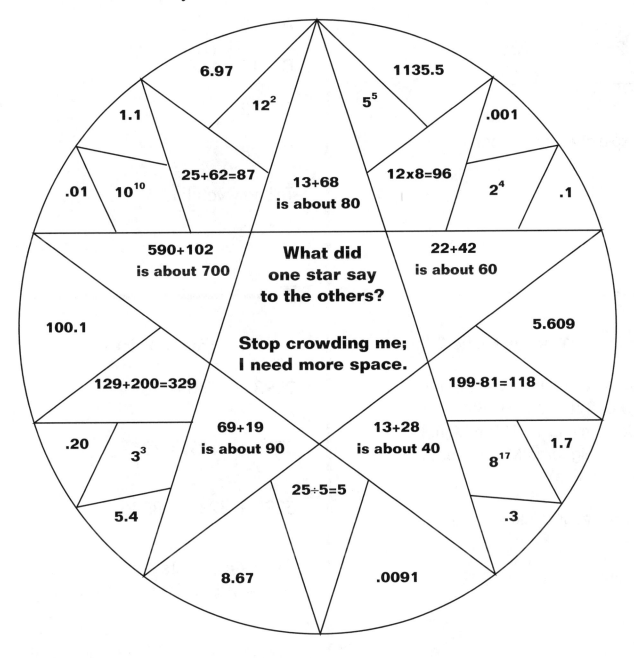

PARENT NOTE:
It is important for students to understand that sometimes an exact answer is not necessary.
Talk with your child about occasions when you have used estimates to make a decision.

Name _____

1

Multiply

110	116
× 10	× 10

230	238
× 10	× 10

Explain your thinking.

2

Find the Missing Divisor

$432 \div$ _____ $= 24$

A   13

B   18

C   22

D   28

Tell how you know.

3

Which Is Higher?

Mt. Everest in Nepal-Tibet is 29,028 ft high. Mt. Shasta in California is 14,162 ft high. How much higher is Mt. Everest than Mt. Shasta?

Show your thinking.

4

True or False?

$2893 + 1748 = 4641$

$3718 + 4129 = 7857$

$5298 + 3247 = 8535$

If any statements are false, write one way to make them true.

▼ PARENT NOTE:
When students examine problems like those in number 4, they can become alert to errors they may make in computing with larger numbers. They will recognize the importance of checking answers.

Find the Quotient

$6 \overline{)1224}$

Show your thinking.

Do You Agree?

Senna chose D as the answer for
$8703 - 4378 =$ _____ .
Do you agree?

A   3325

B   4355

C   4325

D   4435

Explain your thinking.

Chickens and Goats

Farmer Tripp has chickens and
goats in his field. There are
3 times as many chickens as
goats. Farmer Tripp counted
80 legs all together. How many
of the animals are goats? How
many are chickens?

Tell how you know.

True or False?

It took Maria 45 min to make
10 of the thousands blocks. She
keeps working at the same speed.
True or false? It will take her 7 h
to make 100 blocks.

Explain your answer.

Find the Products

2 × 2 = _____

2 × 20 = _____

20 × 20 = _____

20 × 200 = _____

200 × 200 = _____

What can you say about these equations? Write another equation that fits this set.

Complete the Equation

$4.2 - 0.8 =$ _____ $- 2.8$

A   3.4

B   5.0

C   5.2

D   6.2

Explain how you know.

The Answer Is 81

Write 5 subtraction equations that have this answer.

True or False?

On her weekly science tests, Sarbi got scores of 85, 92, 89, 76, and 100. True or false? Her total number of points is 432, and her average is 85.

Show your thinking.

$1,000,000 Dots

Find each answer. Connect the $1,000,000 dots. What shape did
you make?

$$1,000 \times \$1,000 = \text{_____}$$
A •

$$\$10,000 \times 1 = \text{_____}$$
L •

$$10 \times \$100 = \text{_____}$$
• **B**

K •
$$1,000 \times \$100$$

= _____

• **C**
$$100 \times \$1,000$$

= _____

J •
$$10 \times \$10,000$$

= _____

• **D**
$$10 \times \$1,000$$

= _____

I •
$$\$100 \times 10,000$$

= _____

• **E**
$$\$100,000 \times 10$$

= _____

H •
$$\$1,000 \times 1 = \text{_____}$$

• **F**
$$100 \times \$100 = \text{_____}$$

G •
$$100 \times \$10 = \text{_____}$$

What's Your Strategy?
Convince Me!

Martha and Felipe solved the problem 76 × 5 = _____. Look at their solutions. Notice that Martha and Felipe got the same, correct answer, but they used different strategies.

Martha explained her strategy. The teacher recorded it for the class like this:

Felipe used a different strategy. The teacher recorded his explanation like this:

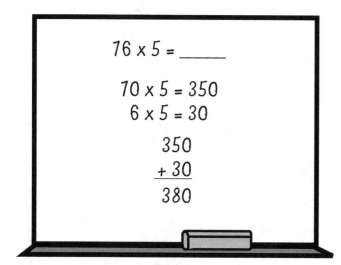

$76 \times 5 =$ _____

$70 \times 5 = 350$
$6 \times 5 = 30$

350
$+ 30$
$\overline{380}$

$76 \times 5 =$ _____

76 x 5 is the same as
$76 \times 10 \div 2$

$760 \div 2 = 380$

Solve the problems below. Record your explanation on paper.

1. $16 \times 5 =$ _____

2. $39 \times 5 =$ _____

3. $81 \times 5 =$ _____

4. $99 \times 5 =$ _____

5. $142 \times 5 =$ _____

6. $283 \times 5 =$ _____

▼1

Find the Sums

0.8 + 2.1 = _____

0.8 + 2.6 = _____

1.7 + 3.1 = _____

1.7 + 3.4 = _____

Explain your thinking.

▼2

Choose the Closest Estimate

378 ÷ 17 = _____

A   10

B   20

C   30

D   40

Show your thinking.

▼3

How Many Crayons?

Ms. Bryant needs to order a box of crayons for every student in the school. There are 7 classes with 31 students each, 4 classes with 33 students each, and 6 classes with 30 students each. How many boxes of crayons does Ms. Bryant need to order?

Tell how you know.

▼4

Agree or Disagree?

Adita filled a jar with 15 scoops of lima beans. She said that it would take 25 of the same-size scoops to fill the same jar with bird seed. Do you agree or disagree?

Explain your thinking.

▼ **PARENT NOTE:**
Estimating is an important skill. While it is especially important in solving division problems, there are many real-life situations that can be solved with an estimate.

Find the Difference

```
  1462
-  378
```

Show your work.

Choose the Best Answer

Marvilla filled $\frac{1}{2}$ c with 45 jelly beans. How many cups would she need for 1,000,000 jelly beans?

A   About 100 cups

B   About 1,000 cups

C   About 10,000 cups

D   About 100,000 cups

Explain your thinking.

How Many Are Wearing Sneakers?

There are 30 students in Ted's class. He noticed that $\frac{3}{5}$ of the students are wearing sneakers today. How many students are wearing sneakers? How many are not wearing sneakers?

Explain how you know.

True or False?

Teri wanted to put her collection of 502 baseball cards into the new book she got for her birthday. There are 32 pages in the book. Each page holds 12 cards. True or false? There are enough pages to hold all of Teri's cards.

Show your thinking.

Name _____

1

Find the Products

20 × 25 = _____

19 × 25 = _____

20 × 35 = _____

19 × 35 = _____

Explain your thinking.

2

Choose the Closest Estimate

An eraser is about 5 cm long. How long would 1,000,000 erasers be placed end to end?

A   200,000 cm

B   50,000 m

C   500,000 m

D   20,000 cm

Tell how you know.

3

The Answer Is 1000

Write 5 multiplication equations that have this answer.

4

Filling the Pantry

Luis and 3 friends collected canned goods for the city food pantry. On different days they collected 143 cans, 119 cans, 167 cans, and 121 cans. How many cans did the students collect all together?

Show your thinking.

PARENT NOTE:
Thinking about a related problem is a powerful computation skill. Problems like number 1 encourage students to take this approach. Students will develop the habit of asking themselves, "What do I know that I can use to solve this problem?"

Plenty of Popcorn

You are given the number of kernels of popcorn in each container. Find how many containers you would need to have 1,000,000 kernels.

Number in Each Container   Number of Containers

1. 400 _____   **A.** 2,000

2. 5,000 _____   **B.** 10,000

3. 500 _____   **C.** 125

4. 100 _____   **E.** 800

5. 8,000 _____   **G.** 250

6. 1,250 _____   **I.** 200

7. 4,000 _____   **K.** 1,000

8. 200 _____   **L.** 20,000

9. 50 _____   **N.** 2,500

10. 250 _____   **R.** 5,000

11. 1,000 _____   **T.** 4,000

Write the letter next to its value to find the answers.

12. The area of this country is about 1,000,000 square miles.

_____ _____ _____ _____ _____ _____ _____ _____ _____
 3   8   7   6   1   10   2   1   3

What's a Good Estimate?
It's Between ...

Build your estimation skills. For each problem, write two numbers, one number that is greater than and one number that is less than the exact answer would be. Explain why you chose those numbers.

$\frac{1}{3}$ of 28

_____ and _____

Why? _____

_____

$\frac{1}{4}$ of 21

_____ and _____

Why? _____

_____

$785 \div 9$

_____ and _____

Why? _____

_____

425×78

_____ and _____

Why? _____

_____

Heather has five bags of popcorn left over from her party. Their weights are 12 oz, 8 oz, 23 oz, 9 oz, and 21 oz. How many ounces of popcorn does she have in all?

The amount of popcorn is between _____ and _____ .

Why? _____

▼ **PARENT NOTE:**
Using estimation is a good way to check if an answer is a reasonable one. Give your child many opportunities to estimate.

1

Subtract

3.4 − 0.9 = _____

3.5 − 1.0 = _____

7.2 − 1.8 = _____

7.4 − 2.0 = _____

Show your thinking.

2

Choose the Correct Answer

$4\overline{)1{,}000{,}000}$

A   250

B   2,500

C   25,000

D   250,000

Tell how you know.

3

1000 Quarters

DeWayne wanted to save 1000 quarters. He discovered that 50 quarters weigh 9 oz. How can DeWayne tell when he has 1000 quarters without counting each quarter?

Explain your thinking.

4

Which Is Greater?

Put < or > in each circle to show which is greater.

28.63 + 7.2 ◯ 28.73 + 7.2

14.08 + 3.9 ◯ 14.8 + 3.09

52.6 + 37.12 ◯ 52.6 + 37.2

Tell how you know.

Multiply

22
×18

Show your thinking.

Choose the Correct Answer

The area of Alaska is 570,374 sq mi. The area of Rhode Island is 1,045 sq mi. How much larger is Alaska than Rhode Island?

A   About 560,000 sq mi

B   Exactly 560,329 sq mi

C   About 569,000 sq mi

D   Exactly 571,419 sq mi

Explain how you know.

Arcade Games

Aman went to the arcade with $7.50. He played 13 games that cost $0.50 each. He bought a drink for $0.63. Does he have enough money to play more games? If so, how many games can he play?

Tell how you know.

Agree or Disagree?

Stacy said that when you divide 742 by 18 the answer is 31 and there is a remainder of 4. Do you agree or disagree?

Explain your thinking.

1

Add

$972.34 + $209.78 = _____

Show your thinking.

2

Choose the Answer

To solve 36 × 28 = _____ which would be false?

A   (18 × 28) + (18 × 28)

B   (3 × 28) + (6 × 28)

C   (36 × 20) + (36 × 8)

D   (30 × 28) + (6 × 28)

Explain how you know.

3

The Answer Is 425

Write 3 subtraction equations each having an answer of 425. Start each equation with 1,000,000.

4

True or False?

4.75 − 2.77 = 2.02

8.62 − 3.65 = 4.97

5.23 − 2.24 = 2.99

If any statements are false, change them to true ones.

▼ PARENT NOTE:
Problems like number 2 ask students to think about the process they use to do arithmetic in different ways. This approach stresses that math should make sense to students and that they should not follow a rule they do not understand.

1,000,000 Equations

Write 6 different equations that have an answer of 1,000,000.
Each equation must have addition, subtraction, multiplication, and
division in it.

Here is an example for 100:

$(50 \div 2) \times 3 - 5 + 30 = 100$

1. _____ = 1,000,000

2. _____ = 1,000,000

3. _____ = 1,000,000

4. _____ = 1,000,000

5. _____ = 1,000,000

6. _____ = 1,000,000

What's an Easy Way?
Computation Review

Solve these problems as quickly as you can. Use the strategies that work best for you.

Circle the pairs of equivalent fractions.

1. $\frac{1}{2}$ and $\frac{2}{3}$

2. $\frac{4}{5}$ and $\frac{16}{20}$

3. $\frac{3}{4}$ and $\frac{8}{10}$

4. $\frac{3}{5}$ and $\frac{6}{10}$

5. $\frac{7}{14}$ and $\frac{8}{16}$

6. $\frac{7}{8}$ and $\frac{8}{9}$

Add.

7. $\frac{1}{9} + \frac{3}{9}$

8. $\frac{1}{5} + \frac{2}{5}$

9. $\frac{3}{10} + \frac{7}{10}$

10. $\frac{1}{2} + \frac{1}{4}$

11. $\frac{1}{5} + \frac{3}{10}$

12. $\frac{1}{4} + \frac{1}{6}$

Solve.

13. $432 + 89$

14. $634 - 298$

15. 43×8

16. $345 \div 5$

17. $912 + 89$

18. $652 - 27$

19. 27×4

20. $299 \div 7$

Name _____

Find the Quotients

$20\overline{)10,000}$

$20\overline{)100,000}$

$20\overline{)1,000,000}$

Explain your thinking.

Which Equation Is False?

A   76 + 24 = 100

B   37 + 73 = 100

C   12 + 88 = 100

D   45 + 55 = 100

Explain how you know.

Science Camp

On Monday Tami's class hiked 1.7 km in the morning and 2.2 km in the afternoon. On Tuesday they hiked 2.75 km, and they hiked 2.69 km on Wednesday. How far did they hike all together?

Tell how you know.

True or False?

Jorge took pictures of his classmates for the school memory book. He used 6 rolls of film that cost $4.76 each. True or false? The total amount spent on film was $29.76.

Explain your answer.

1 Find the Differences

0.1 − 0.01 = _____

0.2 − 0.01 = _____

0.2 − 0.02 = _____

0.3 − 0.02 = _____

Show your thinking.

2 Which Is the Correct Answer?

Lunches at Cedar Street School cost $1.25 each day. How much will Juanita pay if she eats a school lunch 17 times?

A $19.75

B $20.25

C $21.25

D $22.75

Tell how you know.

3 How Far Do You Travel?

At the equator one degree of longitude equals 69.17 mi. If you travel across 4° longitude, how many miles will you travel?

Explain your thinking.

4 True or False?

10 × 100 = 1000

100 × 100 = 100,000

100 × 10,000 = 1,000,000

If any statements are false, write one way to make them true.

PARENT NOTE:
When students make errors in problems like number 1, it is often because of place value. It may help your child to rewrite the problems using zero placeholders; for example, 0.1 − 0.01 is the same as 0.10 − 0.01.

Find the Sum

9428
+1019

Show your work.

Choose the Correct Answer

Which has an answer of 5?

A   4.75 + 1.25 = _____

B   3.05 + 0.95 = _____

C   2.5 + 3.05 = _____

D   2.95 + 2.05 = _____

Explain your thinking.

The Answer Is 37

Write at least 6 subtraction equations that have this answer.

Trees, Trees

Ms. Sheridan wants to plant a row of trees around her property. Her property is a rectangle 84 ft by 60 ft. She will plant a tree every 12 ft. How many trees should she buy?

Tell how you know.

Agree or Disagree?

The teacher gave Shane this problem:

Solve 362 − 179 = _____ .
Explain your answer.

Do you agree or disagree with Shane's work?
Explain your thinking.

362
−179   Write your answer. _____
             Explain how you solved the
                    problem

this is what
the problem looks
like.
   −3 7 9   −3 6 2 switch   −3 | −9 | 7
    1 6 2   1 7 9   −1 | −2 | −6
    2 1 7   2 1 7   2   7   1

First I switch the
2 and the 9. Then I switch
the 6 and the 7 around.
then I left the 3 and 1
alone. I subtracted all of those
and I got 217.

What's Your Strategy?
Convince Me!

Ken and Leonora solved the problem $1.50 + $0.75 = _____ . Look at their solutions.

Notice that Ken and Leonora got the same, correct answer, but they used different strategies.

Ken explained his strategy. The teacher recorded it for the class like this:

Leonora used a different strategy. The teacher recorded her explanation like this:

$1.50 + $0.75 = _____

$1.50 = 1 dollar, 2 quarters
$0.75 = 3 quarters

2 + 3 = 5 quarters = $1.25
$$\begin{array}{r} \$1.25 \\ + 1.00 \\ \hline \$2.25 \end{array}$$

$1.50 + $0.75 = _____

$$\begin{array}{r} \$1.50 \\ + 0.75 \end{array} \qquad \begin{array}{r} \$1.50 \\ .50 \\ + .25 \end{array} \qquad \begin{array}{r} \$2.00 \\ + .25 \\ \hline \$2.25 \end{array}$$

Solve the problems below. Record your explanation on paper.

1. $2.25 + $3.75 = _____

2. $1.75 + $3.75 = _____

3. $3.75 + $2.50 = _____

4. $1.25 + $.75 = _____

5. $4.25 + $2.50 = _____

6. $3.75 + $3.50 = _____

1

Subtract

$3720.21 − $964.70 = _____

Show your thinking.

2

Choose the Correct Answer

Which has the same answer as
3.04 − 0.98 = _____ ?

A   1.78 + 0.38

B   6.56 − 4.9

C   11.64 − 9.68

D   1.09 + 0.97

Tell how you know.

3

Fruit Juice

Ms. Bergren bought 3 cases of fruit juice for $10.87 each. There are 24 bottles in each case. How many bottles of juice did she buy? How much money did she spend?

Explain how you know.

4

True or False?

Neil created a number line for the land area of states. He numbered the line from 2000 square miles to 9000 square miles. He placed the states in the following order: DE (1955 sq mi), CT (4845 sq mi), MA (7838 sq mi), VT (9249 sq mi). True or false? Neil's number line is correct.

Explain your thinking.

Name _____

1

Divide

$25 \overline{)750{,}000}$

$50 \overline{)750{,}000}$

$75 \overline{)750{,}000}$

$100 \overline{)750{,}000}$

Show your thinking.

2

Which Is the Answer?

Marisa bought 2 CDs for $10.67 each and a video tape for $14.49. She gave the clerk $40.00. How much did she receive in change?

A $14.84

B $5.17

C $4.17

D $4.84

Tell how you know.

3

What's the Distance?

Viktor and his brother took a bus trip across the country. They traveled 844 mi from Seattle to Salt Lake City and 1358 mi from Salt Lake City to St. Louis. From St. Louis to Washington, DC, they traveled 835 mi. How far did they travel?

Explain your thinking.

4

True or False?

It is possible to write a true equation with 1.4, 4.2, and 3.

Explain your thinking.

Name _____

1

Find the Sum

```
  2782
+  479
_____
```

Show your thinking.

2

Choose the Correct Answer

Which expression would you use to solve this problem? Farmer LaPlant planted 48 rows of lettuce with 729 plants in each row. How many plants were there in all?

A   729 − 48   C   729 + 48

B   729 × 48   D   729 ÷ 48

Tell how you know.

3

The Answer Is 226

Write at least 5 equations that have this answer. Use addition and subtraction in each equation.

4

True or False?

To put 0.24, 1.02, 0.05, 0.1, and 1.63 on a number line, the number line would need to go from at least 0.5 to 2.

Tell how you know.

What Numbers?

Label each point on each number line. Tell how you decided what to label each point. Which point did you start with? Why? How did that help you figure out the other points?

1.

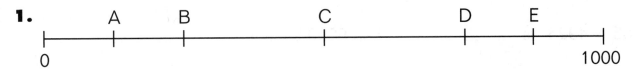

2.

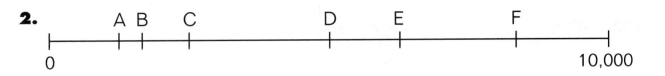

3.

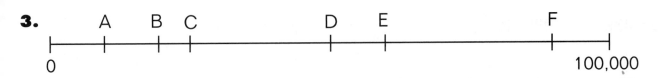

4.

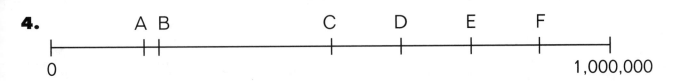

What's a Good Estimate?
Greater Than, Less Than

Build your estimation skills. For each problem, tell if the answer will be less than (<) or greater than (>) the estimate given. Explain why you think so.

1. 2385 + 4925 is _____ than 6000 because _____

_____

2. 55,238 − 46,119 is _____ than 10,000 because _____

_____

3. 45.23 × 9 is _____ than 450 because _____

_____

4. 382.2 ÷ 8 is _____ than 40 because _____

_____

5. 25,439 + 74,982 is _____ than 100,000 because _____

_____

Now, write a problem like one on this page.

▼ **PARENT NOTE:**
Estimating is especially important when working with decimals. Students often misplace the decimal point in their results.

Name _____

Batting Averages

Player	Batting Average
Linda	.286
Maria	.292
Ming	.305
Wendy	.175
Samantha	.225
Elise	.295

Fill in the bubble next to the correct answer.

1. Which list shows the four players with the highest batting averages in order from greatest to least?

○ **A.** Wendy, Samantha, Linda, Maria

○ **B.** Maria, Linda, Samantha, Wendy

○ **C.** Linda, Maria, Elise, Ming

○ **D.** Ming, Elise, Maria, Linda

2. Whose average is greater than Samantha's but less than Maria's?

○ **A.** Elise   ○ **C.** Ming

○ **B.** Linda   ○ **D.** Wendy

3. Whose average has a 2 in the hundredths place?

○ **A.** Linda, Maria, Samantha, and Elise

○ **B.** Maria only

○ **C.** Samantha only

○ **D.** none of these

4. If baseball practice starts at 3:30 and continues for $2\frac{1}{2}$ hours, when will it be over?

○ **A.** 5:00   ○ **C.** 6:00

○ **B.** 5:30   ○ **D.** 6:30

5. The number on Wendy's uniform is a two-digit number that is divisible by 2 and 5 but not by 3 or 4. Which number is it?

○ **A.** 12   ○ **C.** 20

○ **B.** 5   ○ **D.** 50

A Tile Floor

1 sq unit

1. How many square tiles are needed to replace the missing tiles in this floor?

2. Mr. Kent decides to buy 15 new tiles so that he will have extra floor tiles for repairs. If each tile costs $7.50, how much did the new tiles cost?

3. It will take Mr. Kent $2\frac{1}{2}$ hours to repair this floor. He has been working on it from 8:45 until 10:00. How much longer will it take to fix it?

4. Mr. Kent needs 27 inches of floor trim to put across the doorway. He bought 4 feet of floor trim at the store. How much will be left over, in feet and inches.

5. In another room, Mr. Kent is using a pattern of two different colors of tiles. His pattern uses 3 red tiles for every 2 black tiles. If the floor needs 45 tiles in all, how many red tiles will he need? Draw a small section of the floor.

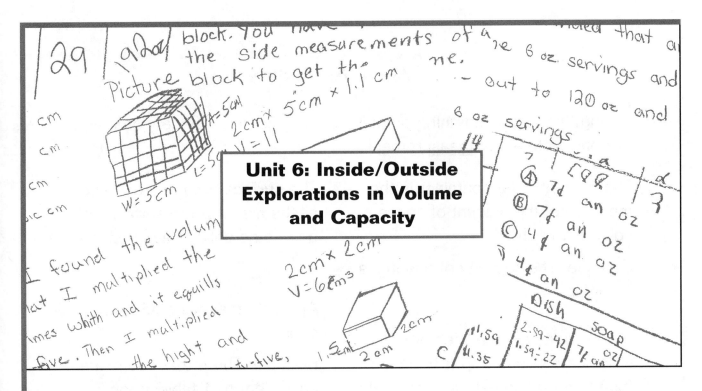

Unit 6: Inside/Outside Explorations in Volume and Capacity

Thinking Questions

What is the largest box you can make beginning with a 20 cm-by-20 cm piece of grid paper? What is the relationship between the dimensions of a box and its volume? Which is the better buy, 42 fl oz for $2.89 or 22 fl oz for $1.59?

Investigations

In this MathLand unit, you will discover answers to these questions and more as your class explores volume and capacity. You will learn how to measure the volume of a rectangular solid, and you will investigate equivalent liquid measures to find the price per ounce.

Real-World Math

Notice the different capacities of food containers in the supermarket. Knowing the price per unit of measure allows customers to find the best buy. Measures of volume are also used in the construction industry to choose the proper type of heating system for a building. What other uses for these types of measurements can you imagine?

Math Vocabulary

During this MathLand unit, you may be using some of these words as you talk and write about measurement.

The **capacity** of a container is the measure of the amount of space or volume it will hold.

Example: The capacity of this jug is 1 gallon.

Calibrations are the lines or marks to indicate values or positions, as found on thermometers, radio dials, and measuring cups.

The **dimensions** of an object show the amount of space an object takes up. The three dimensions are **height**, **length**, and **width**.

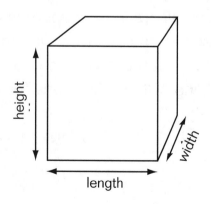

The **surface area** is the sum of all the areas of the surfaces of a geometric solid, measured in square units.

Amounts that are **equivalent**, are equal.

Example: Three teaspoons are equivalent to 1 tablespoon.

A **solid** is a three-dimensional shape.

Volume is the measure of the inside space of a solid. The measure is given in terms of cubic units.

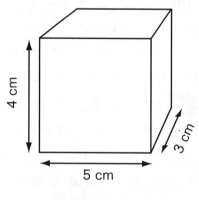

Volume = 60 cm³

Measure Mix-up

Read each statement and write the correct vocabulary word on the blanks.
Unscramble the letters in the boxes to figure out the riddle.

1. 4 cups, 2 pints, and 1 quart are all __ __☐__ __☐__ __ __ __.
T E A E N V L U I Q

2. Length, width, and height are three __ __ __☐__ __ __ __ __☐.
N S N S D M O E I I

3. Lines on a measuring cup are __ __ __ __ __☐__ __ __ __ __ __.
A L B A S N C R I I T O

4. A 2-quart pitcher indicates its __ __☐__ __ __ __.
Y C P A A I T C

5. measured in cubic units __ __ __ __☐__
E M O L V U

6. measured in square units __☐__ __ __ __ __ __ __☐__
R C U E F S A   R E A A

What did the teaspoon say to the tablespoon and cup?

Okay everybody, ☐☐☐☐☐☐☐ ☐☐!

▼ PARENT NOTE:
Measuring skills are useful in many real-life situations. Share
your use of these skills with your child whenever possible.

Name _____

1

Subtract

7802
− 987

Explain your thinking.

2

Which Is the Answer?

Jolynn bought 5 books and a poster. She paid $12.24 for the items. What was the average cost per item?

A $5.04

B $1.72

C $2.04

D $1.62

Tell how you know.

3

How Many Stones?

In Great Britain a person's weight is measured in stones rather than in pounds. About how much would a 100-lb person weigh in stones? One stone is equal to 14 lb.

Show your thinking.

4

True or False?

There are 19 fifth- and sixth-grade students on the school activities committee. There are 5 more sixth-graders than fifth-graders. True or false? There are 5 fifth-grade students and 14 sixth-grade students on the committee.

Explain your answer.

Name _____

1

Find the Products

(Hint: Multiply inside parentheses first.)

$2 \times 4 \times 3 \times 5 =$ _____

$(2 \times 4) \times (3 \times 5) =$ _____

$2 \times (4 \times 3) \times 5 =$ _____

$(4 \times 5) \times (2 \times 3) =$ _____

From these problems, what can you say about multiplying a series of numbers?

2

Choose the Correct Answer

Mr. Gau bought 32 thesauruses for his classroom. He paid $116.48. How much did each book cost?

A $34.24

B $2.94

C $4.09

D $3.64

Tell how you know.

3

How Much Fabric Is Left?

Arelys bought a bolt of fabric to make uniforms and flags. She made 3 uniforms that took 4.15 m of fabric each and 2 flags that took 0.91 m of fabric each. If the bolt had 36.58 m of fabric to start with, how much fabric is left?

Explain how you know.

4

Agree or Disagree?

Isaiah has a box that measures 11 cm by 8 cm by 2 cm. Vince has a box that measures 11 cm by 12 cm by 1 cm. Isaiah said both boxes have the same volume. Do you agree or disagree with Isaiah?

Explain your thinking.

Find the Quotient

$5\overline{)430.5}$

Explain your thinking.

Choose the Correct Answer

The Sugar Sweets Company needs to order boxes to hold sugar cubes. How many 1 cm by 1 cm by 1 cm sugar cubes will fit in a box that measures 8 cm by 7 cm by 3 cm?

A   18 cubes   C   168 cubes

B   56 cubes   D   164 cubes

Tell how you know.

The Answer Is 24 Sq In.

Show at least 4 shapes having an area of 24 sq in.

Solve

Erik wants to stack some boxes on his shelf. The height of the shelf is 42 cm. Erik's boxes have heights of 15.8 cm, 11.3 cm, 8.4 cm, and 9.2 cm. Does he have room to stack all the boxes on top of each other?

Explain your thinking.

Oat Boats Boxes

Oat Boats cereal boxes are 8 in. by 2 in. by 12 in. As the Oat Boat Packaging Manager, you want to ship the cereal to stores in cartons. Each carton should hold 36 boxes of Oat Boats cereal. Make sketches of all the different cartons you could use. Tell the dimensions of each carton. Which carton seems most reasonable? Explain your thinking.

Here is an example of a carton that holds 36 Oat Boats cereal boxes laid end to end.

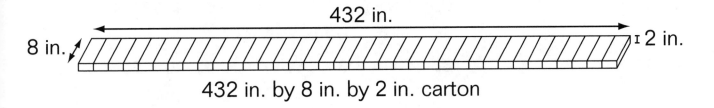

432 in. by 8 in. by 2 in. carton

What's an Easy Way?
Computation Review

Solve these problems as quickly as you can. Use the strategies that work best for you.

Multiply.

1. $25 \times 14 \times 4$ **2.** $17 \times 50 \times 2$ **3.** $5 \times 9 \times 2$

4. $16 \times 3 \times 4$ **5.** $12 \times 10 \times 4$ **6.** $4 \times 31 \times 25$

7. $15 \times 6 \times 2$ **8.** $24 \times 4 \times 3$ **9.** $20 \times 23 \times 5$

Solve.

10. $235 + 258$ **11.** $692 - 38$ **12.** 14×12

13. $389 \div 7$ **14.** $9.23 + 3.2$ **15.** $8 - 2.3$

16. 4.3×6 **17.** $8.05 \div 5$ **18.** 3.072×100

19. $346 - 93$ **20.** $683 + 135$

▼ **PARENT NOTE:**
On this page, students can do many problems mentally if they change the order of the factors. Students who are alert to these choices are comfortable with numbers and confident in their strategies.

Find the Difference

$472.33 − $257.66 = _____

Explain your thinking.

Choose the Answer

A box has a volume of 118.8 cm^3. The length is 4 cm, and the width is 3.3 cm. What is the height?

A   9 cm

B   12 cm

C   6 cm

D   15 cm

Show your thinking.

The Dog Run

Micah's dad wants to fence in a dog run for their new puppy. The run is a rectangle that measures 23 yd by 8.5 yd. How many feet of fence does he need to buy?

Tell how you know.

Agree or Disagree?

Rosa read in her science book that light travels at the speed of 186,281 mi each second. She said that light would travel about 1,000,000 mi in 5 s. Do you agree or disagree?

Explain your thinking.

1

Find the Product

23 × 7 × 8 = _____

Show your thinking.

2

Choose the Correct Answer

There are 206 bones in the body. Each hand has 27 bones. Each foot has 26 bones. How many bones are in the rest of the body?

A   153 bones

B   100 bones

C   163 bones

D   103 bones

Explain your thinking.

3

How Many Went to the Movies?

Rebekah went to the movies with her uncle and 2 brothers and 3 sisters. Each of the girls invited a friend. How many people went to the movies all together?

Explain your answer.

4

True or False?

If a punch cup holds 7 oz, it is possible to get 30 servings from 1.5 gal of punch.
Hint: 128 ounces = 1 gallon

Tell how you know.

Divide

$18\overline{)546}$

$16\overline{)325}$

$17\overline{)681}$

Explain your thinking.

Which Is the Answer?

A box has a length of 6 ft, a width of 9 ft, and a height of 2.4 ft. What is the volume of the box?

A   17.4 ft³

B   129.6 ft³

C   12.96 ft³

D   1296 ft³

Show your work.

The Answer Is 125

Write 5 division equations that have this answer.

Which Is Greater?

Put < or > in each circle to tell which is greater.

8 c $\bigcirc$ 4 qt.

10 c $\bigcirc$ 3 qt.

18 c $\bigcirc$ 3.5 qt.

Hint: 4 cups = 1 quart

Measure Match

Look for 4 equivalent liquid measurements in a row, in a column, or on a diagonal. Can you find all 5 different sets?

2 qt	4 pt	1 gal	64 oz	$\frac{1}{8}$ qt	8 oz	5 pt	1 gal
$\frac{1}{2}$ gal	32 oz	1 qt	2 pt	4 c	6 oz	10 c	$\frac{1}{4}$ qt
8 oz	4 qt	2 gal	3 qt	6 pt	12 c	$\frac{1}{2}$ pt	1 c
2 pt	32 oz	1 gal	8 oz	3 qt	8 oz	8 c	2 pt
4 c	5 qt	16 c	8 pt	1 c	1 gal	4 qt	4 c
8 c	4 qt	8 pt	16 oz	128 oz	3 pt	1 c	32 oz
1 gal	16 pt	128 oz	2 c	2 qt	6 c	16 oz	1 gal
4 qt	$\frac{1}{2}$ gal	7 qt	1 pt	16 oz	2 c	$\frac{1}{2}$ qt	1 pt

What's Your Strategy?
Convince Me!

June and Bill solved the problem $5 \times 18 \times 2 =$ _____ . Look at their solutions. Notice that June and Bill got the same, correct answer, but they used different strategies.

June explained her strategy. The teacher recorded it for the class like this:

Bill used a different strategy. The teacher recorded his explanation like this:

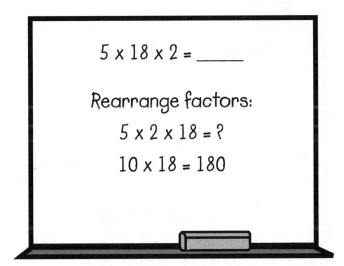

$5 \times 18 \times 2 =$ _____

Rearrange factors:
$5 \times 2 \times 18 = ?$
$10 \times 18 = 180$

$5 \times 18 \times 2 =$ _____

Multiply by 5 last.
$18 \times 2 = 36$
$30 \times 5 = 150$
and $6 \times 5 = 30$
So $36 \times 5 = 180$

Solve the problems below. Record your explanation on paper.

1. $4 \times 12 \times 25 =$ _____

2. $5 \times 7 \times 20 =$ _____

3. $2 \times 36 \times 5 =$ _____

4. $50 \times 8 \times 2 =$ _____

5. $16 \times 4 \times 25 =$ _____

6. $4.3 \times 5 \times 2 =$ _____

▼ **PARENT NOTE:**
When students are able to multiply and divide by 10 and 100, mental computation becomes easier.

Find the Product

$14.38
×   3

Explain your thinking.

Choose the Correct Answer

Andre bought $\frac{1}{2}$ gal of milk. He drank two 8-oz glasses of milk and used 5 oz on his cereal. How much milk was left in the carton? Hint: 128 ounces = 1 gallon

A   21 oz   C   42 oz

B   1 qt   D   1 qt 11 oz

Tell how you know.

Movie Time

Marcia arrives at the movie theater at 3:05. The previews start and take 7 min, the movie runs for 98 min, and there is a short subject that lasts 12 min. What time will Marcia get out of the theater if she leaves after the short subject?

Explain your thinking.

True or False?

The Sears Tower in Chicago is 1454 ft tall. The Civic Opera Building is 555 ft tall. True or false? The Sears Tower is 901 ft taller than the Civic Opera Building.

Show your thinking.

Name _____

Find the Answers

$36 \div 9 =$ _____

$360 \div 9 =$ _____

$360 \div 90 =$ _____

$3600 \div 90 =$ _____

What do you notice about these problems? Write another equation to fit this set.

Which Is the Answer?

How tall is a horse that measures $16\frac{1}{2}$ hands? Horses are measured in hands. Each hand equals 4 in.

A   64 in.

B   46 in.

C $54\frac{1}{2}$ in.

D   66 in.

Show your thinking.

Lemonade

Claire needs to buy lemonade for the fifth-grade picnic. Each 12-oz can of juice makes 48 oz of lemonade. She needs 126 servings. Each serving is 6 oz. How many cans of juice should Claire buy?

Explain your thinking.

True or False?

Trash service in Middletown costs $19.27 per month. True or false? The cost of trash service for one year is $231.24.

Prove it.

▼ PARENT NOTE:
Problems like number 1 encourage students to use patterns for multiplying and dividing multiples of 10.

Find the Answer

12 oz + 23 oz + 1 qt = _____

Show your work.

Choose the Best Answer

$24 \overline{)9264}$

A   Between 200 and 300

B   Between 300 and 400

C   Between 400 and 500

D   More than 500

Explain your thinking.

Your Choice!

Choose a volume. Write the dimensions for 3 different rectangular prisms that have that volume.

Which Is the Better Deal?

Brian bought a 48-oz bottle of juice for $2.88. Lane bought two 16-oz bottles of juice for $2.08. Who got a better deal on his juice?

Tell how you know.

Agree or Disagree?

The teacher gave Raul this problem:

True or False? 88 × 5 = 430
Explain how you know.

Do you agree or disagree with Raul's work?
Explain your thinking.

Explain how you know?
88 × 5 = 430

320

_____

equaled up to false. First I added 88 + 88 and it
be 166. So I added 166 to 166 and
it was 232. then I added 88 to 232 and it
equaled up to 320.

What's a Good Estimate?
It's Between ...

Build your estimation skills. For each problem, write two numbers, one number that is greater than and one number that is less than the exact answer would be. Explain why you chose those numbers.

5.7×2.3

_____ and _____

Why? _____

_____

$29.8 \div 7$

_____ and _____

Why? _____

_____

$65.78 + 307.2$

_____ and _____

Why? _____

_____

$934.9 - 89.25$

_____ and _____

Why? _____

_____

One wall that Linda will paint measures 3.5 meters by 2.6 meters. To find the area of the wall, Linda multiplies 3.5×2.6. What is the answer in square meters?

The area is between _____ sq m and _____ sq m.

Why? _____

▼ PARENT NOTE:
When students write about their estimation strategies, they have opportunities to clarify their thinking and to practice communicating their ideas to others.

Juice in the Fridge

There are four jugs of juice in the refrigerator.

| Apple | Orange | Pineapple | Grape |

Fill in the bubble next to the correct answer.

1. Which chart tells how full each jug is?

- ○ **A.** Apple $\frac{7}{8}$ Orange $\frac{1}{3}$

  Grape $\frac{1}{4}$ Pineapple $\frac{2}{3}$

- ○ **B.** Apple $\frac{7}{8}$ Pineapple $\frac{2}{3}$

  Orange $\frac{1}{4}$ Grape $\frac{1}{2}$

- ○ **C.** Apple $\frac{1}{4}$ Pineapple $\frac{1}{3}$

  Grape $\frac{1}{2}$ Orange $\frac{7}{8}$

- ○ **D.** Apple $\frac{7}{8}$ Grape $\frac{1}{2}$

  Pineapple $\frac{1}{3}$ Orange $\frac{1}{4}$

2. Which two juices could be mixed together in one pitcher and not overflow it?

- ○ **A.** Apple and pineapple
- ○ **B.** Pineapple and grape
- ○ **C.** Orange and grape
- ○ **D.** Grape and apple

3. How many different two-juice combinations are there?

- ○ **A.** 4   ○ **C.** 8
- ○ **B.** 6   ○ **D.** 12

4. If one full jug holds 16 servings, about how many servings of pineapple juice are there?

- ○ **A.** 10   ○ **C.** 14
- ○ **B.** 12   ○ **D.** 16

5. Which fraction is the best estimate of the total amount of juice in all four jugs?

- ○ **A.** $1\frac{1}{2}$ ○ **C.** 2
- ○ **B.** $1\frac{3}{4}$ ○ **D.** $2\frac{1}{4}$

Balancing Boxes of Rice

The small, medium, and large boxes of rice balance each other as shown on these scales.

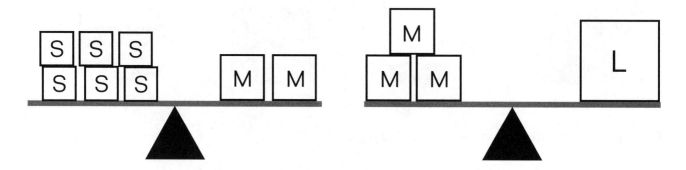

1. How many small boxes of rice hold as much as one medium box?

2. How many small boxes of rice hold as much as one large box?

3. One small box will serve 10 people. How many medium boxes will be needed to serve 75 people?

4. Large boxes cost $5.29 at the supermarket and $6.70 at the corner store. How much will Jim save if he buys the large box at the supermarket.

5. What combination of medium and large boxes will exactly equal the rice in 15 small boxes?

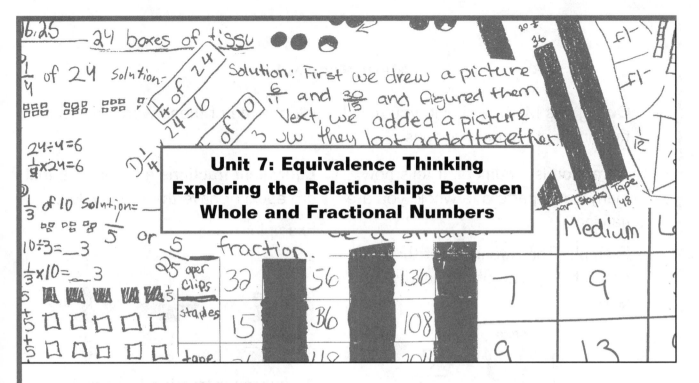

Unit 7: Equivalence Thinking
Exploring the Relationships Between Whole and Fractional Numbers

Thinking Questions

What other familiar fractions are equivalent to $\frac{6}{8}$? Which is greater, $\frac{2}{5}$ or $\frac{2}{3}$? If six of my 27 fish are guppies, what familiar fraction of my fish are guppies?

Investigations

In this MathLand unit, you will discover answers to these questions and more as your class explores the relationships between whole and fractional numbers. You will explore different ways to show the same fraction, and you will learn how to approximate answers to problems using fractions. You will also discover how to compare and order fractional numbers.

Real-World Math

Watch for examples of equivalent fractional numbers on maps and diagrams. Using a scale allows map makers to show distances accurately. Instructions for building models of full-size objects also rely on fractional numbers. Auto mechanics use equivalent fractions to find the correct tools for a job. In what other occupations do you think people use equivalent fractional numbers?

Math Vocabulary

During this MathLand unit, you may be using some of these words as you talk and write about fractions.

A **fraction** is a number. It tells how many equal parts of a whole you are naming.

Example: Three fourths (or three of the four parts) of the sandwich is left.

$$\frac{3}{4}$$

The **numerator** is the top number of a fraction. It means the number of equal parts there are.

The **denominator** is the bottom number of a fraction. It means the number of equal parts something is divided into.

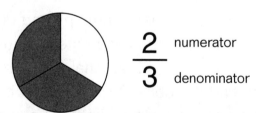

$$\frac{2}{3} \begin{array}{l} \text{numerator} \\ \\ \text{denominator} \end{array}$$

A fraction is in **lowest terms** when 1 is the greatest common factor of both the numerator and the denominator.

Equivalent fractions are fractions that are equal or have the same value.

Example:

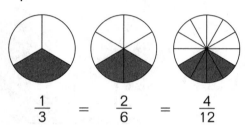

$$\frac{1}{3} = \frac{2}{6} = \frac{4}{12}$$

An **improper fraction** is a fraction whose numerator is larger than the denominator.

Examples: $\frac{12}{2}$, $\frac{9}{4}$

A **mixed number** is a whole number and a fraction.

Examples: $3\frac{1}{4}$, $12\frac{3}{5}$

An **approximation** means "about." The approximation sign ≈ is used to show "about" how much.

Example: $\frac{1}{3} \times 22 \approx 7$ (one third of 22 is about 7)

A **decoy answer** is an incorrect answer used to challenge the person to think carefully.

Duck the Decoys

Read the statements. Cross out all the decoy answers.

1. The numerator is:

the top number of a fraction.

the number of equal parts you have.

the number of equal parts something is divided into.

always less than zero

2. The denominator is:

the top number of an improper fraction.

the bottom number of a fraction.

the number of equal parts.

the number of equal parts something is divided into.

3. Approximation is:

the exact amount.

an educated guess.

"about."

Its symbol is ≈.

4. An improper fraction:

simply has bad manners.

is a fraction with a larger numerator than denominator.

can never equal a whole number.

5. A mixed number:

is a whole number and a fraction.

can be written as an improper fraction.

is confused but very friendly.

6. Cross out the fractions that are not equivalent to the first fraction.

$$\frac{1}{2} = \frac{2}{4} = \frac{4}{8} = \frac{6}{12} = \frac{22}{42} =$$

$$\frac{36}{72} = \frac{54}{106}$$

$$\frac{1}{3} = \frac{4}{12} = \frac{3}{9} = \frac{6}{21} = \frac{7}{24} =$$

$$\frac{9}{36} = \frac{10}{40}$$

7. Decoy answers are:

unfair and are never used.

to challenge students to think.

used mainly to stump people and make their lives miserable.

incorrect.

▼ **PARENT NOTE:**
Encourage your child to explain why he or she chose particular answers for each statement.

1 Find the Quotient

8935 ÷ 15 = _____

Explain your thinking.

2 What's the Weight on Mars?

On Mars people would weigh about $\frac{4}{10}$ what they weigh on Earth. How much would a 150-lb person weigh on Mars?

A   About 20 lb

B   About 40 lb

C   About 60 lb

D   About 80 lb

Show your thinking.

3 Who Saved More?

Bonne saved 10 quarters, 13 dimes, 72 nickels, and 122 pennies. Jonathan saved 9 quarters, 15 dimes, and 68 nickels. Who saved more money? How much more?

Tell how you know.

4 True or False?

Mike and Julie went for a bike ride. They rode for 55 min and then spent 20 min having lunch. They stopped at the library for 45 min and then took 25 min to ride home. They returned home at 2:10 P.M. True or false? It was 11:45 A.M. when they started.

Show your thinking.

Name _____

1

Multiply

$17 \times 3.2 =$ _____

$17 \times 32 =$ _____

$26 \times 2.4 =$ _____

$26 \times 24 =$ _____

Show your work.

2

Choose the Correct Answer

A case of sodas has 24 cans. Each can holds 12 oz. What is the total amount of soda in 1 case? Hint: 32 ounces = 1 quart

A   3 gal

B   3 qt

C   2 gal 1 qt

D   2 gal 2 qt

Explain your thinking.

3

What's Your Story?

Write a story problem for $2617 - 496$.

Show your solution.

4

True or False?

$\frac{1}{4} + \frac{3}{8} = \frac{4}{16} + \frac{6}{16}$

$\frac{1}{3} + \frac{2}{9} = \frac{2}{6} + \frac{1}{6}$

$\frac{1}{5} + \frac{2}{3} = \frac{3}{15} + \frac{6}{15}$

If any statements are false, use > or < to make true ones.

Add

$$\frac{1}{2} + \frac{1}{4} = \underline{\hspace{1cm}}$$

Explain your thinking.

Choose the Closest Estimate

Ramil bought markers for $1.87, paper for $0.79, a pen for $1.39, and a notebook for $3.63. How much did he spend all together?

A $5

B $6

C $7

D $8

Show your thinking.

The Answer Is $\frac{3}{4}$

Write at least 5 equivalent fractions for $\frac{3}{4}$.

True or False?

A package with 2 pens costs $1.26. The Super Pack of pens costs $4.41 for 6 pens and includes 1 free pen. True or false? The cost for each pen is the same in both packs.

Explain how you know.

Name _____

Fraction Match

Draw straight lines to match the equivalent fractions along A and B.
Then match the equivalent fractions along C and D.

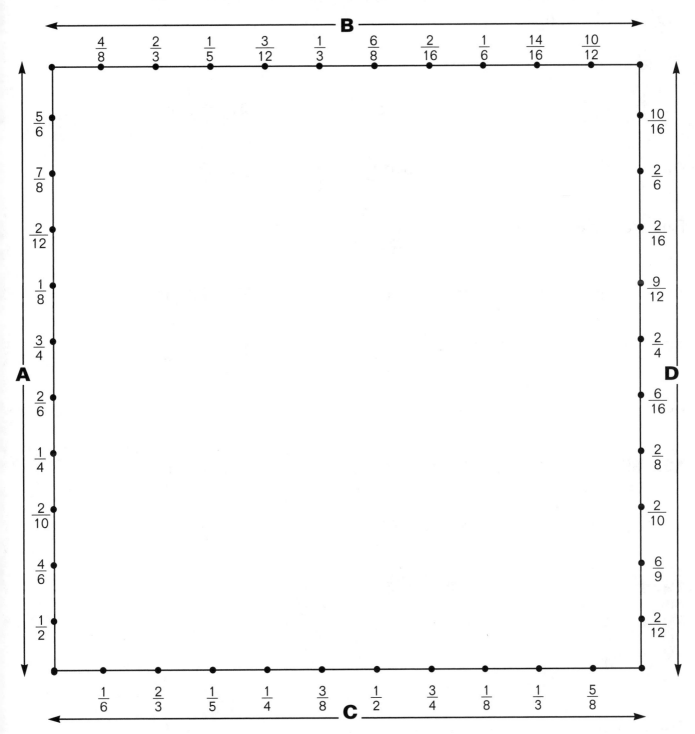

What's an Easy Way?
Computation Review

Solve these problems as quickly as you can. Use the strategies that work best for you.

Circle the equivalent fractions.

1. $\frac{3}{5}$ and $\frac{5}{7}$

2. $\frac{3}{10}$ and $\frac{15}{50}$

3. $\frac{2}{3}$ and $\frac{6}{9}$

4. $\frac{1}{3}$ and $\frac{2}{6}$

5. $\frac{6}{8}$ and $\frac{4}{3}$

6. $\frac{3}{8}$ and $\frac{6}{16}$

Find the missing numerator.

7. $\frac{1}{4} = \frac{}{12}$

8. $\frac{2}{3} = \frac{}{6}$

9. $\frac{4}{5} = \frac{}{15}$

10. $\frac{1}{2} = \frac{}{8}$

11. $\frac{5}{6} = \frac{}{18}$

12. $\frac{1}{3} = \frac{}{9}$

Solve.

13. $789 + 41$

14. $947 - 129$

15. 74×8

16. $828 \div 4$

17. $\frac{2}{3}$ of 21

18. $\frac{3}{4}$ of 100

19. $\frac{1}{3} + \frac{1}{6}$

20. $\frac{2}{7} + \frac{5}{7}$

▼ **PARENT NOTE:**
When students are able to recognize equivalent fractions quickly, they have greater skill in computing with fractions.

Write the Answer

$\frac{1}{8}$ of 48 = _____

Show your thinking.

Choose the Correct Answer

Ms. Singer's class sold 43 bags of popcorn after school. Each bag of popcorn cost $0.50. The class had to pay $2.12 for supplies. How much profit did they make?

A $21.50   C $23.62

B $19.38   D $24.62

Explain your thinking.

How Many Socks Did He Buy?

Darren went to the store to buy socks. A box holds 12 pairs of socks. Darren decided to buy $\frac{2}{3}$ of the box. How many pairs of socks did he buy?

Show how you know.

True or False?

The volume of a box is 190.4 cm^3. The length is 7 cm, and the height is 3.4 cm. True or false? The width is 7 cm.

Prove it.

Name _____

Find the Difference

7958
− 5969

Explain how you know.

Choose the Closest Estimate

$216 + 612 + 126 =$ _____

A   850

B   900

C   950

D   1000

Show your thinking.

Water Molecules

A water molecule lasts 2 weeks in a river. In a large lake a water molecule lasts 10 yr. How many weeks longer does a water molecule last in a lake?

Explain your thinking.

Agree or Disagree?

Maile said that eating $\frac{4}{12}$ of a medium pizza is the same as eating $\frac{9}{36}$ of a medium pizza. Do you agree or disagree?

Tell about your thinking.

Find the Sum

$284.69 + $907.98 = _____

Show your thinking.

Choose the Correct Answer

One yr in a parrot's life is equal to 1 yr 5 mo in a human's life. If a parrot is 11 years old, what would its age be in human years?

A   55 yr

B   11 yr 5 mo

C   5 yr 8 mo

D   15 yr 7 mo

Tell how you know.

The Volume Is 48 Cm³

Show at least 3 different rectangular prisms that have a volume of 48 cm³.

Solve

One of Sheri's dance recital costumes took $1\frac{3}{8}$ yd of trim. Another costume took $2\frac{1}{4}$ yd of trim, and the third costume took $1\frac{1}{2}$ yd of trim. How much trim did the 3 costumes take all together?

Explain your thinking.

Midtown Survey

Elkwood City Council
Elkwood, CA

MEMO

To: City Council Members
Re: Midtown Survey Results

Houses in Midtown

By Color	By Material
White 23	Wood 30
Gray 8	Brick 15
Red 10	Other 3
Blue 5	
Other 2	

Use the survey results to help the Council answer these questions.

About what fraction of all the houses in the Midtown neighborhood are painted each color? Explain your thinking.

1. White   **2.** Gray   **3.** Red

4. Blue   **5.** Some other color

About what fraction of all the houses in the Midtown neighborhood are made of each material? Explain your thinking.

6. Wood   **7.** Brick   **8.** Other

9. The Elkwood City Council will allow 2 more houses to be built in Midtown neighborhood. The houses will be gray and not made of either wood or brick. What fraction of the houses will be gray now? What fraction of the houses will be made of a material other than wood or brick? Explain how you know.

▼ **PARENT NOTE:**
This page gives students practice in getting information from a chart and in determining fractional parts.

What's Your Strategy?
Convince Me!

Marie Clair and Enrico solved the problem $\frac{2}{3} + \frac{1}{4} = $ _____. Look at their solutions. Notice that Marie Clair and Enrico got the same, correct answer, but they used different strategies.

Marie Clair explained her strategy. The teacher recorded it for the class like this:

Enrico used a different strategy. The teacher recorded his explanation like this:

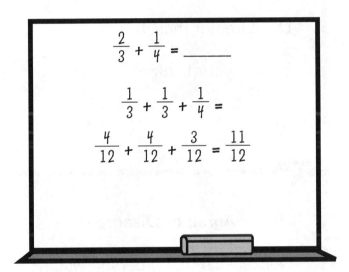

$$\frac{2}{3} + \frac{1}{4} = \underline{}$$

$$\frac{1}{3} + \frac{1}{3} + \frac{1}{4} =$$

$$\frac{4}{12} + \frac{4}{12} + \frac{3}{12} = \frac{11}{12}$$

$$\frac{2}{3} + \frac{1}{4} = \underline{}$$

$$\frac{2}{3} \text{ of } 12 = 8$$

$$\frac{1}{4} \text{ of } 12 = 3$$

$$8 + 3 = 11$$

$$\frac{2}{3} + \frac{1}{4} = \frac{11}{12}$$

Solve the problems below. Record your explanation on paper.

1. $\frac{4}{9} + \frac{1}{3} = $ _____

2. $\frac{1}{5} + \frac{3}{10} = $ _____

3. $\frac{1}{6} + \frac{1}{4} = $ _____

4. $\frac{1}{4} + \frac{1}{2} = $ _____

5. $\frac{1}{2} + \frac{1}{3} = $ _____

6. $\frac{3}{4} + \frac{1}{5} = $ _____

▼ **PARENT NOTE:**
Students are encouraged to talk and write about arithmetic problems in a language that makes sense to them. They will have many opportunities to connect their everyday language to mathematical language and symbols.

Name _____

Write the Answer

$14.62
×   13

Show your thinking.

Choose the Best Answer

$\frac{2}{5} + \frac{3}{7} =$ _____

A   Less than 1

B   Exactly 1

C   About $\frac{1}{4}$

D   Greater than 1

Explain your thinking.

How Many Boat Ramps Are There?

The perimeter of Crystal Lake is 3 mi. There is a boat ramp every $\frac{3}{4}$ mi around the lake. How many boat ramps are there in all?

Tell how you know.

Agree or Disagree?

Denzel said that a person who walks $\frac{7}{12}$ mi goes farther than someone who walks $\frac{5}{8}$ mi. Do you agree or disagree?

Explain your thinking.

1

Solve

$$\frac{3}{4}$$
$$-\frac{1}{8}$$

$$\frac{2}{3}$$
$$+\frac{1}{6}$$

$$\frac{4}{5}$$
$$+\frac{1}{3}$$

$$\frac{7}{9}$$
$$-\frac{1}{4}$$

Show your thinking.

2

Choose the Correct Answer

How would the following fractions be put on a 0–1 number line?

$$\frac{1}{4}, \frac{3}{8}, \frac{1}{2}, \frac{3}{7}, \frac{5}{9}$$

A $\frac{1}{4}, \frac{3}{7}, \frac{3}{8}, \frac{1}{2}, \frac{5}{9}$

B $\frac{1}{4}, \frac{3}{7}, \frac{3}{8}, \frac{5}{9}, \frac{1}{2}$

C $\frac{3}{7}, \frac{1}{4}, \frac{3}{8}, \frac{1}{2}, \frac{5}{9}$

D $\frac{1}{4}, \frac{3}{8}, \frac{3}{7}, \frac{1}{2}, \frac{5}{9}$

Tell how you know.

3

The Daily Schedule

During the day Taiesha is in school from 8 A.M. to 3 P.M. She does homework and has soccer practice from 3 P.M. to 6 P.M. She eats dinner and does chores from 6 P.M. to 8 P.M. From 8 P.M. to 9 P.M. she watches television or reads. What fraction of the day from 8 A.M. to 9 P.M. does Taiesha spend on homework and soccer practice?

Explain your thinking.

4

Getting Change

At the store Mario spent $5.03 for a game, $1.67 for a puzzle, and $0.91 for a sticker. He gave the clerk $10.00. Describe the exact change the clerk may have given to Mario.

Show your thinking.

Name _____

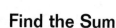

Find the Sum

$$\frac{1}{5} + \frac{2}{3} = \underline{\qquad}$$

Explain your thinking.

Choose the Best Answer

Mr. Wang is going from Detroit to Dallas. Monday he went $\frac{1}{4}$ of the way. Tuesday he went $\frac{1}{3}$ of the remaining distance. It is 1249 mi from Detroit to Dallas. About how much farther does Mr. Wang have to go?

A   425 mi   C   625 mi

B   525 mi   D   725 mi

Explain your thinking.

The Answer Is $\frac{1}{2}$

Write at least 4 addition equations that have this answer.

Buying a Bike

Marika is saving her money to buy a bike. So far she has $143.00. The bike costs $189.00, but it is on sale for $\frac{1}{4}$ off. Does Marika have enough money to buy the bike?

Tell how you know.

Star Quality

Order the fractions from least to greatest to solve each question.

1. What film won the first Academy Award for Best Picture in 1928?

$\frac{1}{3}$	$\frac{5}{6}$	$\frac{3}{8}$	$\frac{1}{4}$	$\frac{7}{10}$
I	S	N	W	G

____ ____ ____ ____ ____

2. In 1982 Richard Attenborough won an Academy Award for Best Director. What film did he direct?

$\frac{2}{3}$	$\frac{4}{12}$	$\frac{5}{8}$	$\frac{5}{6}$	$\frac{10}{24}$	$\frac{1}{4}$
H	A	D	I	N	G

____ ____ ____ ____ ____ ____

3. In 1969 John Wayne won an Academy Award for Best Actor. What film did he star in?

$1\frac{2}{6}$	$\frac{3}{8}$	$1\frac{5}{12}$	$\frac{3}{12}$	$\frac{5}{8}$	$\frac{3}{6}$	$\frac{3}{4}$	$\frac{3}{9}$
I	U	T	T	G	E	R	R

____ ____ ____ ____ ____ ____ ____ ____

4. In 1964 Julie Andrews won an Academy Award for Best Actress. What film did she star in?

$1\frac{1}{6}$	$\frac{1}{9}$	$1\frac{2}{4}$	$\frac{1}{3}$	$\frac{4}{6}$	$\frac{12}{6}$	$\frac{3}{4}$	$\frac{1}{2}$	$\frac{9}{8}$	$1\frac{6}{8}$	$\frac{5}{8}$
P	M	I	A	P	S	O	R	P	N	Y

____ ____ ____ ____ ____ ____ ____ ____ ____ ____ ____

Name _____

What's a Good Estimate?
Greater Than, Less Than

Build your estimation skills. For each problem, tell if the answer will be
less than (<) or greater than (>) the estimate given. Explain why you think so.

1. $\frac{2}{3}$ of 19 is _____ than 12 because _____

_____

2. 48,231 + 23,145 is _____ than 70,000 because _____

_____

3. 3498 − 2612 is _____ than 1000 because _____

_____

4. $\frac{3}{5} + \frac{7}{15}$ is _____ than 1 because _____

_____

5. 3.53 × 12.6 is _____ than 52 because _____

_____

Now, make up your own problem like one on this page.

1

Write the Answer

$\frac{2}{3}$ of 36 = _____

Show your thinking.

2

Choose the Correct Answer

Gabe and his dad walk 3.75 mi every night. How can you find the total distance they walked in May?

A 31 ÷ 3.75

B 31 × 3.75

C 31 + 3.75

D 31 − 3.75

Tell how you know.

3

Wood to Burn

Mr. Ho bought 5 cords of wood to burn in the fireplace. Each cord of wood measures 3.62 m^3. If Mr. Ho burned 2 cords of the wood, how many cubic meters of wood were left?

Explain your thinking.

4

True or False?

$\frac{2}{3} + \frac{5}{9} = 1\frac{7}{12}$

$\frac{4}{5} + \frac{1}{2} = 1\frac{3}{10}$

$\frac{3}{4} + \frac{5}{6} = 1\frac{3}{4}$

If any statements are false, make them true.

▼ **PARENT NOTE:**
In problems like number 2, students are asked to think about only the method that makes sense and not to find the exact answer.

Find the Difference

1062 − 978 = _____

Explain your thinking.

Choose the Correct Answer

Mr. Lewis bought two $\frac{1}{2}$-gal cartons of milk. How many 12-oz servings are in the 2 cartons?
Hint: 32 ounces = 1 quart

A Fewer than 8 servings

B About 8 servings

C About 10 servings

D More than 12 servings

Tell how you know.

At the Circus

There are 1284 people at the circus. There are $\frac{1}{2}$ as many adults as children. How many adults are at the circus? How many children?

Explain how you know.

True or False?

If 1 bale of cotton weighs 227.1 kg, then 6 bales of cotton weigh 1362.6 kg.

Explain your thinking.

Multiply

$19 \times 34 =$ _____

$38 \times 34 =$ _____

$76 \times 34 =$ _____

Show your thinking.

What's the Sum?

Choose the correct answer.

$$\frac{2}{3} + \frac{3}{4} = \text{_____}$$

A $\frac{5}{12}$

B $1\frac{6}{12}$

C $\frac{5}{7}$

D $1\frac{5}{12}$

Explain how you know.

The Answer Is 0.5

Write at least 6 equations that have this answer.

Solve

Robert wants to store his videos in a box that measures $14\frac{3}{4}$ in. by $8\frac{1}{4}$ in. by 2 in. Each video case measures $7\frac{3}{8}$ in. by $4\frac{1}{8}$ in. by 1 in. How many videos can he store in the box?

Explain your thinking.

Agree or Disagree?

The teacher gave Aiko this problem:

Anna has a paper route. She delivers 128 papers every weekday.
She delivers 172 papers on Saturday and 172 papers on Sunday.
How many papers does she deliver in 1 week? In 4 weeks?
Tell how you know.

Do you agree or disagree with Aiko's work?
Explain your thinking.

128 papers
172 papers
+ 172 papers
472 papers in one week
X 4 weeks
1,888 papers in four weeks

First I added the number of papers Anna delivered on weekday to the number of papers she delivered on Saturday and Sunday, that gave me the number of papers in a week. Then I multiplied the number of papers in a week by 4 and got the number of papers in four weeks. Just to make sure I was right I checked myself with a calculator.

What's an Easy Way?
Computation Review

Solve these problems as quickly as you can. Use the strategies that work best for you.

Add.

1. $\dfrac{1}{5} + \dfrac{2}{5}$

2. $\dfrac{1}{6} + \dfrac{1}{6}$

3. $\dfrac{3}{8} + \dfrac{1}{8}$

4. $\dfrac{1}{2} + \dfrac{1}{4}$

5. $\dfrac{1}{5} + \dfrac{3}{10}$

6. $\dfrac{1}{6} + \dfrac{2}{3}$

Subtract.

7. $\dfrac{7}{8} - \dfrac{1}{8}$

8. $\dfrac{8}{9} - \dfrac{1}{9}$

9. $\dfrac{4}{5} - \dfrac{1}{5}$

10. $\dfrac{3}{4} - \dfrac{3}{8}$

11. $\dfrac{1}{2} - \dfrac{1}{4}$

12. $\dfrac{5}{6} - \dfrac{1}{12}$

Solve.

13. $2672 + 4994$

14. $5032 - 1734$

15. 32×5

16. $5409 \div 9$

17. $45.6 + 7.38 + 12.8$

18. $68.7 - 3.49$

19. 76×3

20. $2748 \div 6$

▼ **PARENT NOTE:**
Estimating is also useful when working with fractions. Students can think of fractions as close to 0, 1/2 or 1. Encourage your child to explain to you how he or she estimates answers.

Name _____

Find the Sum

$$\dfrac{5}{8}$$
$$+\,1\dfrac{1}{4}$$

Show your thinking.

Choose the Best Answer

There are 32 students in Mr. Pawah's class. Seven of the students walk to school. About what fraction of the class walks to school?

A   About $\dfrac{1}{8}$ C   About $\dfrac{1}{3}$

B   About $\dfrac{1}{5}$ D   About $\dfrac{1}{2}$

Explain your thinking.

What's the Change?

At the mall Tamika spent $3.76 for a bracelet, $14.39 for a shirt, and $2.12 for a pair of socks. She gave the clerk $25. What are 2 different ways the clerk can make Tamika's change?

Explain your thinking.

Which Is Greater?

Put < or > in each circle to make a true statement.

$\dfrac{2}{7} + \dfrac{5}{12}$ ◯ $\dfrac{2}{7} + \dfrac{1}{2}$

$\dfrac{1}{3} + \dfrac{1}{4}$ ◯ $\dfrac{1}{3} + \dfrac{1}{8}$

$\dfrac{1}{5} + \dfrac{1}{7}$ ◯ $\dfrac{1}{6} + \dfrac{1}{8}$

Explain your thinking.

Name _____

Find the Sums

$$\begin{array}{r} \$1029.07 \\ +\quad 286.99 \\ \hline \end{array} \qquad \begin{array}{r} \$1029.06 \\ +\quad 287.00 \\ \hline \end{array}$$

$$\begin{array}{r} \$2045.18 \\ +\quad 732.97 \\ \hline \end{array} \qquad \begin{array}{r} \$2045.15 \\ +\quad 733.00 \\ \hline \end{array}$$

Show your thinking.

Write another set of problems like these.

Choose the Correct Answer

$36.06 + 9.97 =$ _____

A   460.3

B   46.03

C   260.3

D   36.03

Tell how you know.

Tons of Trash

According to a recent survey, every person creates an average of 1460 lb of trash each year. Suppose each person in your family throws away the average amount of trash. What is your family's total amount of trash for the year? Make a list of items you could recycle.

Explain your thinking.

Which Is Greater?

Put < or > in each circle to show which is greater.

$1\frac{7}{8} - \frac{3}{4}$ $\bigcirc$ $1\frac{7}{8} - \frac{5}{8}$

$1\frac{2}{3} - \frac{2}{9}$ $\bigcirc$ $1\frac{2}{3} - \frac{1}{3}$

$1\frac{3}{4} - \frac{1}{2}$ $\bigcirc$ $1\frac{3}{4} - \frac{5}{8}$

Explain how you know.

1

Find the Product

$6.7 \times 14 =$ _____

Explain your thinking.

2

Choose the Best Answer

Lake Michigan is about 923 ft deep. About what is its depth in fathoms? One fathom equals 6 ft.

A   About 100 fathoms

B   About 125 fathoms

C   About 150 fathoms

D   About 175 fathoms

Show your thinking.

3

The Answer Is 2

Use fractions to write 3 different equations that have this answer.

4

True or False?

535 nickels = $26.85.

48 quarters = $12.00

326 nickels = $16.30

If any statements are false, make them true.

Spending Money

You earned $5.00 for walking the neighbor's dog. You want to decide what to buy among these items.

Comic Book
$1.25

Nuts
$0.50

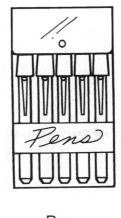

Pens
$2.50

Orange Juice
$0.75

1. Which item is $\frac{1}{2}$ of your money?

2. Which item would take $\frac{1}{4}$ of your money?

3. Which 2 items together are $\frac{1}{4}$ of your money?

4. Suppose you buy everything but the pens. What fraction of your money would you spend?

5. Suppose you buy the comic book and the juice. What fraction of your money would you spend?

6. Suppose you buy the comic book and the set of pens. What fraction of your money would you spend?

7. Decide what items you would buy. What is the total cost? What fraction of your total money did you spend?

What's Your Strategy?
Convince Me!

Abby and Mike solved the problem $1\frac{1}{4} - \frac{3}{8} =$ _____. Look at their solutions. Notice that Abby and Mike got the same, correct answer, but they used different strategies.

Abby explained her strategy. The teacher recorded it for the class like this:

$$1\frac{1}{4} - \frac{3}{8} = \underline{\hspace{1cm}}$$

$$1 - \frac{3}{8} = \frac{5}{8}$$

$$\frac{5}{8} + \frac{1}{4} = \frac{5}{8} + \frac{2}{8}$$

$$= \frac{7}{8}$$

Mike used a different strategy. The teacher recorded his explanation like this:

$$1\frac{1}{4} - \frac{3}{8} = \underline{\hspace{1cm}}$$

$$\frac{5}{4} - \frac{3}{8} = \frac{10}{8} - \frac{3}{8}$$

$$= \frac{7}{8}$$

Solve the problems below. Record your explanation on paper.

1. $2\frac{1}{6} - \frac{2}{3} =$ _____

2. $1\frac{1}{5} - \frac{3}{10} =$ _____

3. $1\frac{1}{3} - \frac{1}{2} =$ _____

4. $3\frac{1}{4} - \frac{5}{6} =$ _____

5. $1\frac{2}{5} - \frac{3}{4} =$ _____

6. $1\frac{1}{6} - \frac{1}{2} =$ _____

▼ **PARENT NOTE:**
Students are encouraged to develop their own strategies for solving problems. After considering other strategies, they may decide to use them as presented or develop yet another approach.

A Trip to the Lake

The lake is 10 miles from the campsite. Leon started out on foot. $2\frac{1}{2}$ hours later, Mike started on his bicycle. This graph shows their progress.

Fill in the bubble next to the correct answer.

1. Which statement is true?

   ○ **A.** Neither boy got to the lake.

   ○ **B.** Mike got to the lake before Leon.

   ○ **C.** Leon got to the lake before Mike.

   ○ **D.** They got to the lake at the same time.

2. How long a rest did Leon take during his hike?

   ○ **A.** 0 minutes   ○ **C.** 1 hour

   ○ **B.** 30 minutes   ○ **D.** 2 hours

3. If Leon left the campsite at 8:00 am, when did he get to the lake?

   ○ **A.** 12:00   ○ **C.** 4:00 pm

   ○ **B.** 12:30 pm   ○ **D.** 4:30 pm

4. When did Leon walk fastest?

   ○ **A.** During the first hour.

   ○ **B.** After the first hour.

   ○ **C.** After the second hour.

   ○ **D.** After the third hour.

5. If Mike continued at the same speed, in how many hours would he be 30 miles from the campsite?

   ○ **A.** 3 hours   ○ **C.** 4 hours

   ○ **B.** $3\frac{1}{2}$ hours   ○ **D.** $4\frac{1}{2}$ hours

Name _____

The School Band

This circle graph shows how different instruments make up the school band.

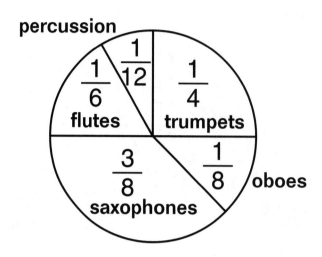

There are 48 band members in all.

1. How many band members play percussion?

2. What fraction of the band members play flute or oboe?

3. How many more band members play saxophone than play trumpet?

4. Jeannette, Latoya, Maria and Tracey will play a saxophone quartet at the next concert. In how many different ways can they be arranged on stage from left to right?

5. Next month, the band will get two more members. Both of them play saxophone. What fraction of the band will play saxophone then?

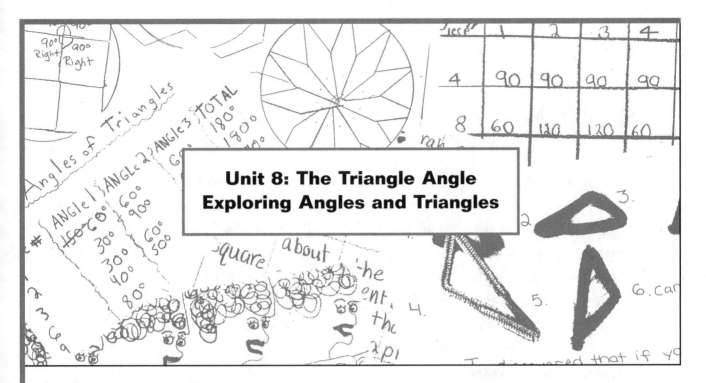

Thinking Questions

Can a triangle have two right angles? What is the sum of all the angles of a five-sided polygon? What is an obtuse angle? Can you form a triangle using lengths of 15 cm, 5 cm, and 5 cm?

Investigations

In this MathLand unit, you will discover answers to these questions and more as your class explores angles and triangles. You will investigate the angles inside polygons, and you will discover the relationships between the side lengths of triangles. You will also explore which polygons will tessellate a plane, and you will create unique tessellation designs.

Real-World Math

Look for ways in which the triangle is used in construction and design. Bridges are often strengthened with supports using this shape. Games we play are sometimes based on a design made of triangles. What other examples of geometric shapes do you find in your everyday life?

Math Vocabulary

During this MathLand unit, you may be using some of these words as you talk and write about geometry.

An **angle** is made up of two rays or line segments having a common endpoint. Angles are measured in **degrees**. Angles that measure 90° are called **right angles**. **Acute angles** measure less than 90°, and **obtuse angles** measure more than 90°. The degrees of an angle can be measured by a **protractor.**

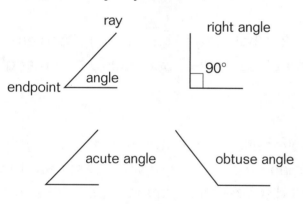

A triangle has three angles. A **right triangle** is a triangle with one 90° angle. An **acute triangle** is a triangle with three angles each less than 90°. An **obtuse triangle** has one angle that is greater than 90°.

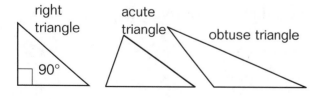

A triangle also has three sides. The sides of an **equilateral triangle** are all equal. An **isosceles triangle** has two equal sides. The **scalene triangle** is a triangle with no equal sides.

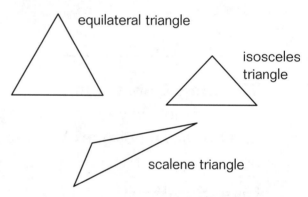

Tessellating means covering a space completely with repetitions of one shape or a combination of shapes.

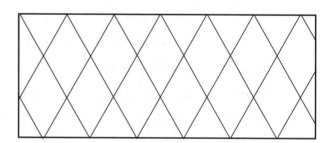

Geometric Design

Color each right triangle in the design green. Color each trapezoid red. Color each parallelogram blue. Color each obtuse triangle yellow.

Make your own design in the grid below using three or more shapes listed in this unit's vocabulary words. Write down what each shape should be colored. Then color the design or give it to a classmate to color.

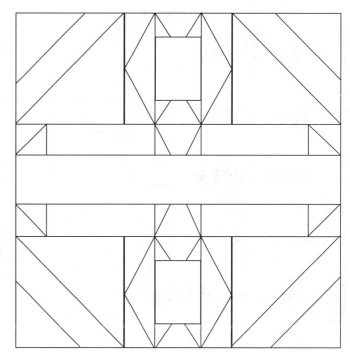

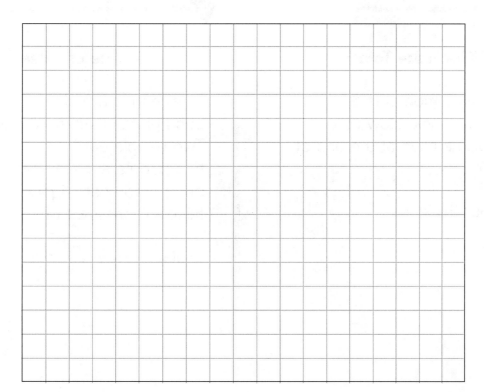

PARENT NOTE:
Ask your child to explain the way he or she has named each type of figure.

Name _____

1

Subtract

$1007 - 788 =$ _____

$1019 - 800 =$ _____

$2642 - 386 =$ _____

$2656 - 400 =$ _____

Explain your thinking.

2

Find the Divisor

$5304 \div$ _____ $= 312$

A   15

B   17

C   170

D   150

Tell how you know.

3

What's the Total?

Every week Simon puts $1.25 into his coin bank. How much money will he have at the end of the year?

Show your thinking.

4

True or False?

Five friends are sharing 2 pizzas. Each pizza is cut in 10 pieces. Two people eat 3 pieces each, two people eat 2 pieces each, and one person eats 4 pieces. True or false? There is $\frac{7}{10}$ of a pizza left.

Explain how you know.

1

Find the Sums

1015 + 999 = _____

1014 + 1000 = _____

7167 + 998 = _____

7165 + 1000 = _____

Show your thinking.

2

Choose the Correct Answer

Suni rode her bike $5\frac{1}{3}$ mi to visit a friend. How many feet did she ride? There are 5,280 ft in 1 mi.

A   26,400 ft

B   24,640 ft

C   28,260 ft

D   28,160 ft

Tell how you know.

3

Carnival Time

Last year the school carnival brought in $4872 for field trips. This year the carnival brought in $\frac{1}{6}$ more money. How much money did the carnival make this year?

Explain your thinking.

4

Rain, Rain

The normal annual rainfall in Miami, Florida, is about 54 in. What is the average rainfall for each month?

Show your thinking.

Divide

782.7 ÷ 6 = _____

Show your thinking.

Choose the Correct Answer

Valerie has 3 hr between school and dinner. She spends 1 hr 40 min babysitting, 12 min eating, 55 min doing homework, and 4 min changing clothes. How much time is left to ride her bike?

A   2 hr 51 min   C   9 min

B   1 hr 51 min   D   49 min

Explain your thinking.

The Answer Is 16

Write at least 5 subtraction equations that have this answer.

How Much Did He Spend?

On Saturday Marshall spent $\frac{1}{2}$ dollar, $\frac{1}{4}$ dollar, $\frac{2}{5}$ dollar, and $\frac{7}{10}$ dollar. What is the total value of the money he spent?

Tell how you know.

Name _____

Missing Angle Measures

Find the missing angle measure. Tell whether it is a right, an acute, or an obtuse angle.

1.
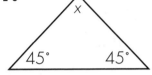

4.

7.
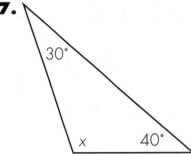

2.
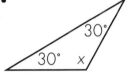

5.
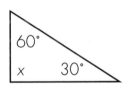

8.
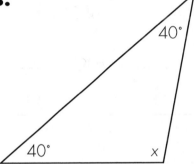

3.
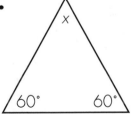

6.
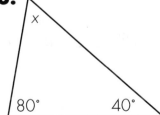

9.
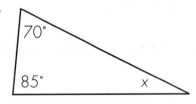

What's a Good Estimate?
It's Between ...

Build your estimation skills. For each problem, write two numbers, one number that is greater than and one number that is less than the exact answer would be. Explain why you chose those numbers.

$45.26 \div 12$

_____ and _____

Why? _____

_____

$2812.7 \div 7$

_____ and _____

Why? _____

_____

$\frac{3}{4}$ of 21

_____ and _____

Why? _____

_____

$\frac{9}{10}$ of 16

_____ and _____

Why? _____

_____

Wesley wants 4 square yards of carpeting that costs $18.99 per square yard. How much will it cost?

The cost of the carpeting will be between $ _____ and $ _____ .

Why? _____

▼ PARENT NOTE:
Estimation skills are very important. Share with your child situations in your own life in which you estimate. Ask your child to explain how he or she estimates a result.

Name _____

1

Find the Product

27 × 18 = _____

Explain your thinking.

2

Find the Missing Addend

2378 + _____ = 2640

A   262

B   252

C   225

D   264

Tell how you know.

3

Spring Flowers

Mrs. Diaz planted 48 spring flowers in her garden. One fourth of the flowers are pansies, $\frac{1}{6}$ are petunias, $\frac{2}{8}$ are marigolds, and $\frac{1}{3}$ are snapdragons. How many of each kind of flower did Mrs. Diaz plant?

Show your thinking.

4

Agree or Disagree?

Ian's test scores are 74, 72, 81, 79, and 86. He said if he gets an 84 on the next test, his average will be 80. Do you agree or disagree?

Explain your thinking.

Name _____

Add

$$\frac{3}{10}$$
$$\frac{1}{2}$$
$$+ \frac{2}{5}$$
_____

Explain your thinking.

Find the Missing Factor

$16 \times 7 \times$ _____ $= 1232$

A   9

B   10

C   11

D   12

Tell how you know.

Great Lakes

The water surface area of Lake Superior is 31,700 sq mi. The area of Lake Erie is 9,910 sq mi. How much larger is Lake Superior than Lake Erie?

Show your thinking.

True or False?

Everything in the store is $\frac{1}{4}$ off. The regular prices of 3 items are $7.88, $4.96, and $12.64. True or false? The total sale cost of these items is $18.76.

Explain your thinking.

1

Find the Products

$27 \times 2.8 =$ _____

$54 \times 1.4 =$ _____

$32 \times 5.6 =$ _____

$64 \times 2.8 =$ _____

Explain your thinking.

2

Choose the Answer

Andrew divided a circle into 11 equal sections. How many degrees are in each section?

A   Fewer than 30°

B   Exactly 32°

C   A little more than 32°

D   More than 33°

Show your thinking.

3

The Answer Is $\frac{2}{3}$

Write at least 3 subtraction equations that have this answer.

4

Agree or Disagree?

On Saturday Tomas hiked $4\frac{1}{3}$ mi. On Sunday he hiked $4\frac{3}{5}$ mi. Tomas said he hiked farther on Saturday than on Sunday. Do you agree or disagree?

Explain your thinking.

Name _____

Secret Message

Write the answer. Some letters have values. Write these letters in the boxes with their values. Find the secret message.

A. A triangle with one 90° angle ___ ___ ___ ___ ___
32 6 9 13

B. To find the sum of two numbers, you would . . . ___ ___ ___
1 24 29

C. A triangle with one angle greater than 90° ___ ___ ___ ___ ___
4   26 11

D. A triangle with all angles less than 90° ___ ___ ___ ___ ___
7   17 33

E. 49 ÷ 7 = ___ ___ ___ ___ ___
15   36

F. A triangle with sides of different lengths ___ ___ ___ ___ ___ ___ ___
40   14 10 25 8 20

G. A triangle with two sides of equal length

___ ___ ___ ___ ___ ___ ___ ___
22   21 2 39 12

H. 400 × 2 = ___ ___ ___ ___ ___   ___ ___ ___ ___ ___ ___ ___
37 18   31   28   19 16

I. A triangle with three sides of equal length

___ ___ ___ ___ ___ ___ ___ ___ ___ ___
34   23 3 27 30 5 35 38

1	2	3		4	5	6	7	8	9	10	11
12		13	14	15	16		17	18	19	20	21
	22	23	24	25	26		27	28	29		30
31	32	33	34		35	36	37	38	39	40	

170 Skill Power • 5   © Creative Publications

What's an Easy Way?
Computation Review

Solve these problems as quickly as you can. Use the strategies that work best for you.

Add. Write your answer in lowest terms.

1. $2\frac{1}{2} + 1\frac{1}{4}$ **2.** $3\frac{2}{3} + 1\frac{5}{6}$ **3.** $4\frac{1}{5} + 2\frac{3}{10}$

4. $2\frac{3}{4} + 1\frac{7}{8}$ **5.** $1\frac{5}{8} + 1\frac{1}{2}$ **6.** $3\frac{1}{3} + 2\frac{2}{9}$

Subtract. Write your answer in lowest terms.

7. $1\frac{5}{6} - \frac{2}{3}$ **8.** $2\frac{3}{4} - 1\frac{1}{2}$ **9.** $4\frac{2}{3} - 2\frac{1}{9}$

10. $2\frac{1}{8} - \frac{1}{2}$ **11.** $1\frac{1}{6} - \frac{1}{4}$ **12.** $3\frac{2}{5} - 1\frac{7}{10}$

Solve.

13. $38.7 + 29.6$ **14.** $2091 \div 3$ **15.** 6.2×7

16. $45.5 \div 5$ **17.** $\$20 - \$14.50$ **18.** $\frac{3}{5}$ of 50

19. $22.3 + 76.1$ **20.** 3.6×9

1

Find the Sum

94.78 + 6.2 = _____

Show your thinking.

2

Choose the Best Answer

An adult Asian elephant can weigh 13,000 lb. An adult giant tortoise can weigh 870 lb. How much more does the elephant weigh?

A   About 12,000 lb

B   Exactly 1,230 lb

C   About 5,000 lb

D   Exactly 13,230 lb

Explain your thinking.

3

Wheels, Wheels, Wheels!

Enrique counted 60 wheels at the city park obstacle course. There were skateboard and bicycle riders on the course. There were 3 times more bicycles than skateboards. How many skateboards were at the competition? How many bicycles were there?

Explain how you know.

4

True or False?

The bank machine shows that Mrs. Kuriyama's balance is $1067.28. She deposits $486.33. True or false? Her new balance is $1553.61.

Tell how you know.

1

Find the Product

32.4
×   8

Explain your thinking.

2

Choose the Best Answer

$$3\frac{8}{15} - 1\frac{2}{7}$$

A   About $3\frac{1}{2} - 1\frac{1}{4}$

B   About $3\frac{1}{4} - 1\frac{1}{4}$

C   About $3\frac{1}{3} - 1\frac{1}{3}$

D   About $3\frac{2}{3} - 1\frac{1}{3}$

Show your thinking.

3

How Many Passengers?

In one year the leading airline flew 84,813 passengers. Another airline flew 1,388 passengers during the year. How many more passengers did the leading airline carry?

Tell how you know.

4

A Complete Circle

Fatikh placed shapes around a center dot. The shapes he had in place had angles of 60°, 20°, 35°, and 90°. How many more degrees does he need to make a complete circle around the center dot?

Explain how you know.

Name _____

1 Subtract

1411 − 693 = _____

1418 − 700 = _____

3212 − 197 = _____

3215 − 200 = _____

Show your thinking.

Explanations will vary.

2 Choose the Answer

Which gives the closest estimate for 7269 × 4876?

A 7000 × 5000

B 7000 × 4000

C 8000 × 5000

D 8000 × 4000

Explain your thinking.

3 The Answer Is 0.75

Show at least 3 subtraction equations that have this answer.

4 Pencils for All

Ms. Luna wants to buy award pencils for her students. The pencils come in packages of 5 for $1.19. How many packages will she need for 33 students? How much will the pencils cost all together?

Tell how you know.

▼ **PARENT NOTE:**
In problems like number 3, there are many possible correct answers. Students show their understanding of the number and of subtraction when they create three different equations with this answer.

Name _____

What Tessellates?

Mr. Arman wants to put in a new tile floor in his bathroom. He wants a pattern that tessellates. You work for Tidy Tiles. Which pattern would you suggest Mr. Arman get for his bathroom? Explain your thinking.

1.

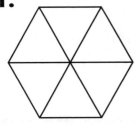

Jewel

4.

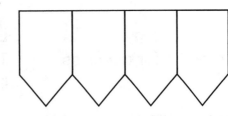

Picket Fence

2.

Windmill

5.

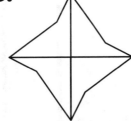

Star Gazer

3.

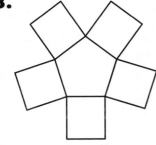

Ferris Wheel

6.

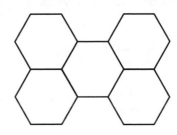

Honeycomb

Mr. Arman decides he wants something different. He wants you to design a new tile pattern that tessellates. Design a new tile pattern for Mr. Arman's bathroom floor.

What's Your Strategy?
Convince Me!

Cindy and Luke solved the problem 180 − (24 + 63) = _____ . Look at their solutions. Notice that Cindy and Luke got the same, correct answer, but they used different strategies.

Cindy explained her strategy. The teacher recorded it for the class like this:

Luke used a different strategy. The teacher recorded his explanation like this:

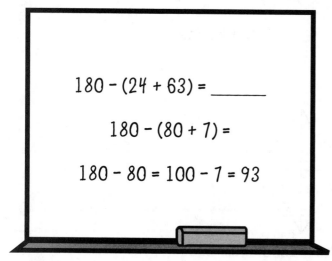

$180 - (24 + 63) =$ _____

$180 - (80 + 7) =$

$180 - 80 = 100 - 7 = 93$

$180 - (24 + 63) =$ _____

$$
\begin{array}{r}
180 \quad +3 = 183 \\
\underline{-87} \quad +3 = \underline{-90} \\
93
\end{array}
$$

Solve the problems below. Record your explanation on paper.

1. 180 − (45 + 35) = _____

2. 180 − (37 + 49) = _____

3. 180 − (72 + 36) = _____

4. 180 − (120 + 23) = _____

5. 180 − (95 + 40) = _____

6. 180 − (136 + 15) = _____

Name _____

Find the Sums

$\frac{2}{9} + 1\frac{1}{3} =$ _____

$\frac{1}{3} + 1\frac{1}{3} =$ _____

$\frac{4}{9} + 1\frac{1}{3} =$ _____

$\frac{5}{9} + 1\frac{1}{3} =$ _____

Write the next equation in this series.

Find the Missing Addend

$8\frac{1}{9} +$ _____ $= 14\frac{2}{3}$

A $5\frac{1}{6}$

B $4\frac{5}{9}$

C $5\frac{4}{9}$

D $6\frac{5}{9}$

Tell how you know.

How Much Turf Is Needed?

The grounds crew needs to order turf to resurface the lawn area. The area measures 12 yd by $5\frac{1}{3}$ yd. How many square feet of turf do they need?

Show how you know.

True or False?

The United States Mint prints paper money in sheets of 32 bills per sheet. True or false? The value of 5 sheets of $5.00 bills is $1000.00.

Explain your thinking.

Add

7156
+3579

Show your thinking.

Choose the Correct Answer

It costs about 1¢ per hour to burn a 100-watt incandescent light bulb. It costs 1¢ to burn a 27-watt fluorescent bulb for 4 hours. How much more does it cost to burn an incandescent bulb than a fluorescent bulb for 100 hours?

A $75   C $0.75

B $0.55   D $0.73

Tell how you know.

How Many Muffins Are There?

Irina went to the bakery for muffins. She bought $\frac{1}{2}$ dozen blueberry muffins, $\frac{2}{3}$ dozen poppyseed muffins, and $\frac{1}{6}$ dozen apple muffins. How many muffins did she buy all together?

Explain your thinking.

Water Use

In the highest water-use state, each person uses an average of 275 gal of water each day. In the lowest water-use state, each person uses an average of 98 gal of water each day. In one week how many more gal of water does a person in the high-use state use than a person living in the low-use state?

Show your thinking.

Name _____

Find the Difference

2662 − 1485 = _____

Show your thinking.

Choose the Correct Answer

The class gave a performance of *Annie.* Adult tickets cost $5.25 each. Child tickets cost $3.00 each. There were 12 adults and 34 children at the play. How much money did they collect for tickets?

A $165.00   C $122.40

B $184.00   D $238.10

Explain your thinking.

The Answer Is 0

Show 3 equations that have this answer. Use only fractions in your equations.

True or False?

Mrs. Chou had 1 lb of dried fruit. She ate $\frac{3}{16}$ lb. Her daughter ate $\frac{1}{4}$ lb, and her son ate $\frac{1}{8}$ lb. True or false? There are 9 oz of dried fruit left.
Hint: 16 ounces = 1 pound

Explain how you know.

Agree or Disagree?

The teacher gave Merdad this problem:
Choose the correct answer.

$4.36 − $0.88 = _____

A $5.24   C $3.58

B $2.58   D $3.48

Explain how you know.

Do you agree or disagree with Merdad's work?
Explain your thinking.

$4.36
−$0.88
$3.48

$5.24 This answer can not be because it is higher than the dollars we are subtracting from.

B.2.58 This answer is not the correct one because it is too low to just subtract 88.¢

C. This answer and D might be the right one so I have decided to do the problem.

The correct one is D

What's a Good Estimate?
Greater Than, Less Than

Build your estimation skills. For each problem, tell if the answer will be
less than (<) or greater than (>) the estimate given. Explain why you think so.

1. 68.3 + 42.1 is _____ than 100 because _____

_____

2. 794.7 − 283.2 is _____ than 500 because _____

_____

3. 43.5 × 6 is _____ than 300 because _____

_____

4. 289.7 ÷ 5 is _____ than 50 because _____

_____

5. $\frac{1}{2}$ of 395 is _____ than 200 because _____

_____

Now, make up your own problem like one on this page.

What's an Easy Way?
Computation Review

Solve these problems as quickly as you can. Use the strategies that work best for you.

Add.

1. 4.2 + 7.9

2. 1.94 + 6.23

3. 15.8 + 37.3

4. 6.2 + 3.18

5. 43.5 + 2.76

6. 63.45 + 71.9

Multiply.

7. 3.2 × 7

8. 5.9 × 4

9. 6.3 × 8

10. 2.3 × 9

11. 7.6 × 3

12. 9.1 × 6

Solve.

13. 4527 + 1783

14. 8621 − 3788

15. 43 × 8

16. 4368 ÷ 4

17. $\frac{1}{2} + \frac{2}{3}$

18. $\frac{4}{5} - \frac{1}{10}$

19. 5.4 − 1.8

20. 6.9 − 1.23

Name _____

A Divided Triangle

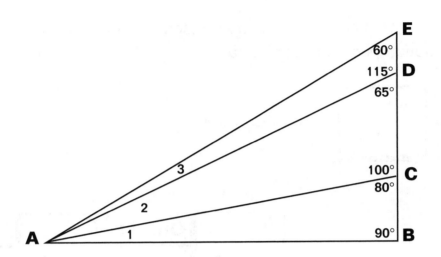

Fill in the bubble next to the correct answer.

1. How many different triangles are shown in this diagram?

○ **A.** 3   ○ **C.** 6

○ **B.** 4   ○ **D.** 9

2. What is the measure of angle 1?

○ **A.** 10°   ○ **C.** 80°

○ **B.** 60°   ○ **D.** 170°

3. Which triangles are obtuse? (Hint: Triangles are named by their vertices.)

○ **A.** ACD only

○ **B.** ACD and ADE only

○ **C.** ACD, ACE and ADE

○ **D.** ABC, ACD, ACE and ACE

4. Which sentence can be used to find the measure of ∠3?

○ **A.** 180 − 120

○ **B.** 180 − 115 − 60

○ **C.** 60 − ∠1 − ∠2

○ **D.** 90 − ∠1 − ∠2

5. The area of triangle ABC is 2/3 the area of triangle ADE. If the area of triangle ADE is 9 square centimeters, what is the area of triangle ABC?

○ **A.** 2 sq cm   ○ **C.** 4 sq cm

○ **B.** 3 sq cm   ○ **D.** 6 sq cm

┌─ ▼**PARENT NOTE:** ──────────────
│ Students can use the problems on this page as
│ a practice test in geometry and geometric terms.
└──────────────────────────────────

Number Machines

This diagram shows three connected number machines. Each machine performs the operation printed under its name.

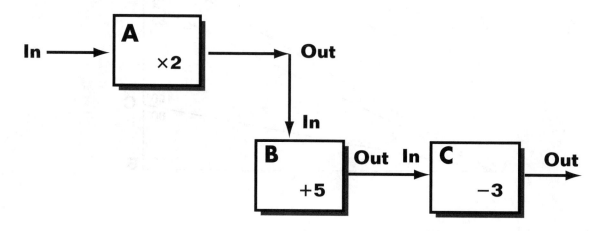

1. If the number 6 is put in Machine A, what number will come out of Machine A?

2. If the number 3 is put in Machine A, what number will come out of Machine B?

3. If the number 5 is put in Machine A, what number will come out of Machine C?

4. What number must be put into Machine A in order to get 24 from Machine C?

5. Machine D is attached to Machine C. This table shows the results of numbers that go through Machine D. Look at the table and tell what rule Machine D uses.

In	Out
10	14
18	22
26	30
42	46

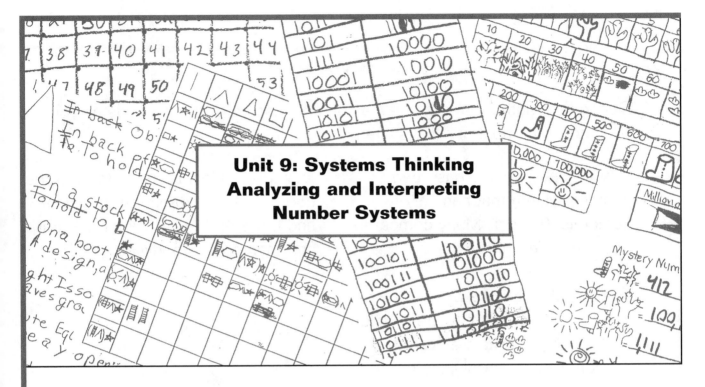

Unit 9: Systems Thinking
Analyzing and Interpreting
Number Systems

Thinking Questions

What is a negative number? What happens when you add two negative numbers? What is a binary number? How can you design your own number system?

Investigations

In this MathLand unit, you will discover answers to these questions and more as your class analyzes and interprets number systems. You will explore different number systems, and you will learn to record numbers using the binary number system.

Real-World Math

Watch for ways that number systems are used to create codes in everyday life. The supermarket uses a code for food products, which identifies each product and its price. Banks use codes to provide access to services and accounts. Games we play are sometimes based on secret codes. What other uses for number systems can you imagine?

Math Vocabulary

During this MathLand unit, you may be using some of these words as you talk and write about number systems.

A **binary** system is a base two number system that has only two numerals, 0 and 1. Many computers operate under this system.

The **coordinates** of a point are a set of numbers that identify the location of the point. A **grid** is a system of horizontal and vertical lines forming squares that are of equal size. Grids are used as a reference for locating points. To find a point on a grid, look at the coordinates. The second coordinate gives the point's horizontal (or sideways) location and the second coordinate gives the point's vertical (or up and down) location.

Example: To locate the point with the coordinates (3, 4) on the grid, you find the 3 on the horizontal line first, and then count up 4 lines.

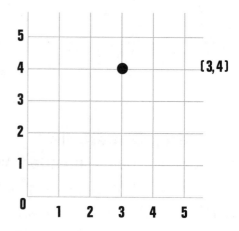

An **integer** is a positive or negative whole number or zero.

Examples: −9, 0, 22

A **negative number** is a number less than 0.

A **positive number** is a number greater than 0.

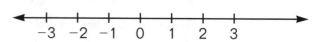

Name _____

Use Your Grid!

Use the grid below to answer the questions.
In some questions you will also have to write the coordinates.
To find the letter of a coordinate, the first number tells the horizontal
location and the second number tells the vertical location.

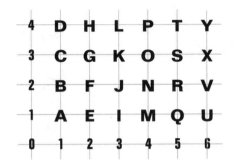

1. A ___ ___ ___ ___ ___ ___ system is a base 2 number system.
   (1,2) (3,1) (4,2) (1,1) (5,2) (6,4)

2. A ___ ___ ___ ___ is a pattern of horizontal and vertical lines forming
   (2,3) (5,2) (3,1) (1,4)
   squares of the same size.

3. A ___ ___ ___ ___ ___ ___ ___ ___ number is greater than 0.
   (4,4) (4,3) (5,3) (3,1) (5,4) (3,1) (6,2) (2,1)

4. A ___ ___ ___ ___ ___ ___ ___ ___ number is less than 0.
   (4,2) (2,1) (2,3) (1,1) (5,4) (3,1) (6,2) (2,1)

5. Some examples of ___ ___ ___ ___ ___ ___ ___ ___ ___ ___ ___
   are (5,2) and (2,0). (1,3) (4,3) (4,3) (5,2) (1,4) (3,1) (4,2) (1,1) (5,4) (2,1) (5,3)

6. A positive or negative whole number is an ___ ___ ___ ___ ___ ___ ___.
   (3,1) (4,2) (5,4) (2,1) (2,3) (2,1) (5,2)

Use the grid above to write a secret message.

1

Subtract

$4763.65
− 935.89

$4763.76
− 936.00

$5124.52
− 711.85

$5124.67
− 712.00

Show your thinking.

Write another set of problems like these.

2

Choose the Correct Answer

In 1973 *Skylab 4* spent 2017 h 15 min in space. About how many days was the *Skylab 4* mission?

A   70 d

B   80 d

C   90 d

D   100 d

Tell how you know.

3

Granola

Jarmila wants to make some granola. The recipe calls for $1\frac{2}{3}$ c of oatmeal. She wants to double the recipe. How much oatmeal does she need?

Show your thinking.

4

True or False?

$6 - 4.03 = 2.97$

$7 - 2.05 = 4.95$

$8 - 5.04 = 3.96$

If any statements are false, change them to true ones.

▼ **PARENT NOTE:**
Problems like number 3 may come up in your home. It would be helpful to your child to know how you approach a problem like this one.

Find the Quotient

$8\overline{)3584}$

Explain your thinking.

Choose the Correct Answer

There are 3 tennis balls packed in 1 can. A case holds 24 cans. How many tennis balls are there in 12 cases?

A   288 tennis balls

B   60 tennis balls

C   72 tennis balls

D   864 tennis balls

Tell how you know.

Movie Time!

On Saturday there were 183 boys and girls at the movie theater. There were 9 more boys than girls. How many boys were at the movie? How many girls were at the movie?

Show your thinking.

True or False?

A sperm whale dives about 1500 ft. A dolphin dives about $\frac{2}{3}$ as deep as a sperm whale. True or false? A dolphin dives about 500 ft.

Explain how you know.

Write the Answers

$8 + {}^{-}3 =$ _____

$4 + {}^{-}3 =$ _____

$3 + {}^{-}3 =$ _____

$2 + {}^{-}3 =$ _____

Show your thinking.

Choose the Correct Answer

It costs 67¢ to dry a load of clothes in an electric clothes dryer. It costs 16¢ to dry a load of clothes in a gas dryer. How much money does a person save by drying 16 loads of clothes in a gas dryer?

A	$0.51	C	$8.16
B	$10.72	D	$13.28

Tell how you know.

The Answer Is $\frac{3}{8}$

Write at least 5 equations that have this answer.

The 800-m Run

In 1896 Edwin Flack completed the 800-m run in 2 min 11 s. In 1984 Joaquin Cruz ran the 800-m in 1 min 43 s. How much faster did Mr. Cruz run than Mr. Flack?

Show your thinking.

Crack the Code

Ms. Stewart's printer has scrambled the day's math problems.
She needs your help to crack the code and to solve the problems.

1. Which symbol represents each of the numbers from 0 to 9?

β = _____ ϖ = _____ ε = _____ ρ = _____ κ = _____

ϕ = _____ ψ = _____ χ = _____ o = _____ λ = _____

Use the following problems to help you crack the code.

2. ϕ × ϕ = ϕ

_____ × _____ = _____

3. χ + χ = o

_____ + _____ = _____

4. ϖ – ϕ = ϕ

_____ – _____ = _____

5. ϖ + χ = ε

_____ + _____ = _____

6. ϖ × ϖ = ψ

_____ × _____ = _____

7. β – ε = χ

_____ – _____ = _____

8. ε – ψ = ϕ

_____ – _____ = _____

9. ρ – ε = ϖ

_____ – _____ = _____

10. ϕ κ κ – λ λ = ϕ

_____ _____ _____ – _____ _____ = _____

Use the code to solve these problems. Write your answers in numerals.

11. $\phi\, o$ × β = _____

12. $\phi\,\kappa\,\varepsilon\,\varpi$ + $\chi\, o\,\lambda$ = _____

13. $\varepsilon\,\beta\,\psi$ – $\chi\,\lambda\, o$ = _____

14. $\phi\,\rho$ – ψ + β – ϖ = _____

© Creative Publications

Skill Power • 5 **191**

What's Your Strategy?
Convince Me!

Sou-kan and Melinda solved the problem $\frac{1}{3}$ of 10 = _____. Look at their solutions. Notice that Sou-kan and Melinda got the same, correct answer, but they used different strategies.

Sou-kan explained his strategy. The teacher recorded it for the class like this:

$\frac{1}{3}$ of 10 = _____

$\frac{1}{3}$ of 10 = $\frac{1}{3}$ of (9 + 1)

$\frac{1}{3}$ of 9 = 3

$\frac{1}{3}$ of 1 = $\frac{1}{3}$.

So, $\frac{1}{3}$ of 10 = $3\frac{1}{3}$

Melinda used a different strategy. The teacher recorded her explanation like this:

$\frac{1}{3}$ of 10 = _____

$\frac{1}{3}$ of 10 is between $\frac{1}{3}$ of 9

and $\frac{1}{3}$ of 12.

$\frac{1}{3}$ of 9 = 3, $\frac{1}{3}$ of 12 = 4.

9, 10, 11, 12

10 is $\frac{1}{3}$ of the distance between 9 and 12.

So, $\frac{1}{3}$ of 10 = $3\frac{1}{3}$.

Solve the problems below. Record your explanation on paper.

1. $\frac{1}{2}$ of 21 = ——

2. $\frac{1}{5}$ of 32 = ——

3. $\frac{1}{3}$ of 17 = ——

4. $\frac{1}{4}$ of 30 = ——

5. $\frac{1}{6}$ of 25 = ——

6. $\frac{1}{2}$ of 19 = ——

▼ **PARENT NOTE:**
Students' use of more than one strategy to solve a problem shows good number sense and confidence in the ability to solve a wide variety of problems. It is important for students to realize that there is usually more than one way to get a correct answer.

Name _____

Find the Difference

2704 − 1348 = _____

Explain your thinking.

Choose the Correct Answer

The distance by air from Los Angeles to New York City is 2451 mi. If a plane flies from Los Angeles at a speed of 520 mi per hour, how long will it take to reach New York City?

A   1931 h   C   About 3 h

B   About $4\frac{1}{2}$ h   D   About 6 h

Show your thinking.

What's Your Story?

Write a story problem for 5729 + 853.

Show your solution.

Agree or Disagree?

Ivar has 11 bills in his pocket. He has one-dollar, five-dollar, and ten-dollar bills. The total value of the bills is $49. Do you agree or disagree? Ivar has 3 ten-dollar bills, 3 five-dollar bills, and 4 one-dollar bills in his pocket.

Tell how you know.

1

Write the Answer

$$\begin{array}{r} 471 \\ \times\ \ 7 \\ \hline \end{array}$$

Show your thinking.

2

Choose the Correct Answer

A cheese sandwich has 1548 mg of sodium, and a pickle has 928 mg of sodium. If you eat $\frac{1}{3}$ of the sandwich and $\frac{1}{2}$ of the pickle, how much sodium do you eat?

A   1496 mg   C   1506 mg

B   1032 mg   D   980 mg

Explain how you know.

3

Babysitting

Anad babysat for his neighbors and earned $2.50 an hour. On Saturday he babysat for $5\frac{1}{2}$ h and on Sunday he babysat for 7 h. How much money did he earn?

Tell how you know.

4

True or False?

7113 + 2997 = 10,110

5002 + 1998 = 7000

1401 + 3999 = 4400

If any statements are false, write one way to make them true.

Write the Answer

1.04 − 0.23 = _____

Explain your thinking.

Choose the Answer

An L-1011 airplane uses 2384 gal of fuel each hour it flies. How much fuel does the plane burn in a 4-h flight?

A   9536 gal

B   8536 gal

C   9236 gal

D   9226 gal

Tell how you know.

The Answer Is 49

Write at least 6 equations that have this answer.

True or False?

Lenae rode her bike 1 mi the first week, 2 mi the second week, 4 mi the third week, 7 mi the fourth week, and 11 mi the fifth week. True or false? At this rate, she will ride her bike 15 mi the sixth week.

Show your thinking.

Name _____

What's Next?

Look at the patterns of the shapes below. What shape comes next in each series?
Draw each shape in the empty box.

1.

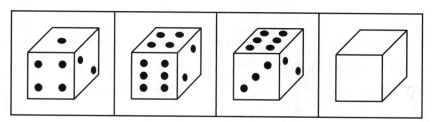

2.

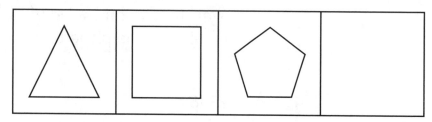

3.

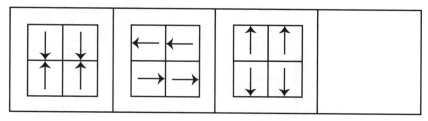

4.

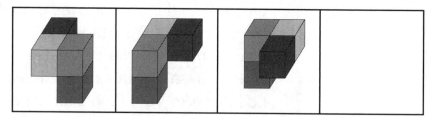

5. Make your own series of shapes. Show the solution.

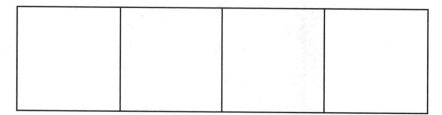

What's a Good Estimate?
It's Between ...

Build your estimation skills. For each problem, write two numbers, one number that is less than and one number that is greater than the exact answer would be. Then explain why you chose those numbers.

56 × 38

_____ and _____

Why? _____

_____

29 × 73

_____ and _____

Why? _____

_____

493 ÷ 12

_____ and _____

Why? _____

_____

891 ÷ 28

_____ and _____

Why? _____

_____

A space mission spent 1782 hours in space. How many days was this?

The number of days is between _____ and _____ .

Why? _____

Name _____

Find the Product

49
× 23

Explain your thinking.

Choose the Correct Answer

For which would you use
$74.89 − $24.96?

A   Have $74.89, get $24.96.

B   Have $74.89, spend $24.96.

C   Spend $24.96, then spend
     $74.89.

D   Have $49.93, spend $24.96.

Tell how you know.

Super Bowl III

The total number of points scored
in the 1969 Super Bowl was 23.
The New York Jets beat the
Baltimore Colts by 9 points. What
was the final score of the game?

Show your thinking.

True or False?

Roberto wants to make $\frac{1}{2}$ of a
cookie recipe. The whole recipe
calls for $1\frac{1}{2}$ c of flour. True or
false? To make $\frac{1}{2}$ of the recipe,
Roberto should use $\frac{2}{3}$ c of flour.

Show how you know.

Find the Sum

```
  0.65
+ 0.87
```

Show your thinking.

Choose the Best Answer

The Empire State Building is 1250 ft tall. It has 102 stories. What is the average height for each story?

A   Less than 11 ft high

B   About 12 ft high

C   About 14 ft high

D   More than 15 ft high

Explain your thinking.

Is It Enough?

Simone has $10.00 to spend at the store. She needs to buy 2 cartons of milk for $1.03 each, 1 loaf of bread for $1.79, a box of cereal for $3.29, and 4 lb of apples that cost $0.59 a lb. How can she estimate to know if she has enough money?

Show your thinking.

True or False?

A mouse's heart beats 624 times per minute. True or false? It beats 17,820 times in 30 min.

Tell how you know.

1

Write the Answer

$$3\frac{1}{8} + 8\frac{3}{16} = \underline{\hspace{1cm}}$$

Show your thinking.

2

Choose the Best Answer

Which of the following has the same answer as $4.06 - 1.87$?

A $3.87 + 0.18$

B $0.87 + 2.19$

C $4.19 - 2$

D $6.87 - 4.86$

Tell how you know.

3

The Answer Is 96 Cm²

Show at least 5 different shapes having this area.

4

How Much Higher?

The highest point in Louisiana is Driskill Mountain with an elevation of 535 ft. The lowest point is New Orleans with an elevation of −8 ft. How much higher is the elevation of Driskill Mountain?

Explain how you know.

Name _____

Finish the Base 3 Number Chart to show the numbers 1–30.

Base 3 Number Chart

27	9	3	1	
			1	1
			2	2
		1	0	3
		1	1	4
		1	2	5
				6
				7
				8
				9
				10
				11
				12
				13
				14
				15
				16
				17
				18
				19
				20
				21
				22
				23
				24
				25
				26
				27
				28
				29
				30

Name _____

What's an Easy Way?
Computation Review

Solve these problems as quickly as you can. Use the strategies that work best for you.

Add.

1. $23.45 + $15.89

2. $35.25 + $72.76

3. $43.18 + $38.24

4. $456.23 + $287.56

5. $2,378.35 + $8,129.25

6. $325.89 + $609.52

Subtract.

7. $86.99 − $25.38

8. $24.19 − $8.24

9. $65.27 − $41.38

10. $345.67 − $218.34

11. $4,398.23 − $1,289.73

12. $756.38 − $495.63

Solve.

13. 74 × 6

14. 83.5 × 3

15. 34.5 ÷ 5

16. $\frac{1}{2} + \frac{1}{4}$

17. $\frac{7}{9} - \frac{1}{6}$

18. $\frac{1}{3}$ of 22

19. 62.1 ÷ 3

20. $\frac{1}{5}$ of 63

Name _____

Add

```
  512
  325
+ 917
```

Show your thinking.

Find the Missing Factor

$7 \times$ _____ $\times 4 = 448$

A   14

B   15

C   16

D   17

Explain how you know.

Junk in Space!

Debris from satellites and space ships travels through space at a speed of 17,500 mi per hour. How far would a piece of "junk" travel in 15 min?

Tell how you know.

Agree or Disagree?

Halil said that $3\frac{7}{30} + 1\frac{6}{11}$ is greater than 6. Do you agree or disagree?

Explain your thinking.

Name _____

Find the Difference

10,528
− 2,613

Show your thinking.

Choose the Correct Answer

Ms. Fong has $55 to spend on plants. Each plant costs $6.47. How many plants can she buy?

A   8 plants with $0 left over

B   8 plants with $3.00 left over

C   8 plants with $3.14 left over

D   8 plants with $3.24 left over

Tell how you know.

How Many Cups?

Each school day Craig eats $\frac{3}{4}$ c of cereal with $\frac{1}{2}$ c of milk. How many cups of cereal does Craig eat in 1 school week? How many cups of milk does he use on his cereal?

Show how you know.

Which Is Greater?

Put < or > in each circle to make a true statment.

30.01 + 2.99 ◯ 20.9 + 10.09

45.01 + 1.99 ◯ 45.9 + 1.01

52.9 + 2.01 ◯ 52.9 + 2.1

Tell how you know.

Find the Product

198 × 12 = _____

Show your thinking.

Choose the Correct Answer

Mr. Jai's heart beats 103,689 times per day. He breathes 23,040 times each day. How many more heart beats than breaths does Mr. Jai's body make in a day?

A   9,351   C   126,729

B   80,649   D   70,649

Explain your thinking.

The Answer Is 1.2

Write at least 4 subtraction equations that have this answer.

True or False?

In 1973 a gallon of gas cost $0.39. In 1990 a gallon of gas cost $1.15. True or false? In 1990 it cost $9.22 more for 12 gal of gas than it did in 1973.

Tell how you know.

The Line System

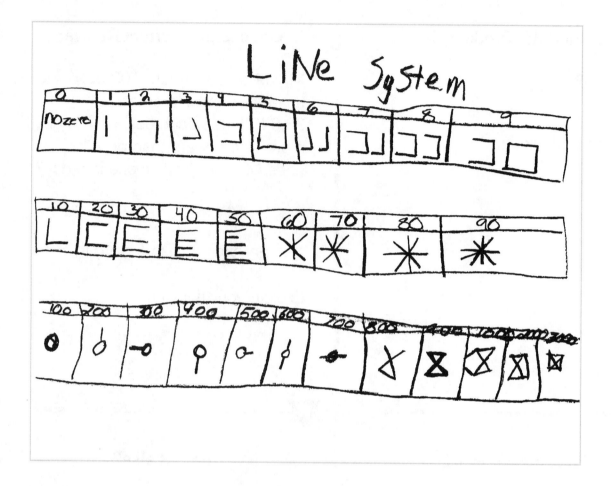

The "Line System" is a number system developed by a pair of fifth-grade students. Use their system to rewrite and to solve the following problems.

1. 123 + 69 = _____

3. 87 ÷ 9 = _____

2. 3425 − 1809 = _____

4. 430 × 8 = _____

5. Were you able to use the "Line System" to solve every problem? If not, why not?

6. What are the advantages of this system? What are the disadvantages?

7. What suggestions do you have to improve this number system?

8. Write a problem of your own using the "Line System." Show your solution.

What's Your Strategy?
Convince Me!

Ben and Carla solved the problem 13 × 25 = _____ . Look at their solutions. Notice that Ben and Carla got the same, correct answer, but they used different strategies.

Ben explained his strategy.
The teacher recorded it for the class like this:

Carla used a different strategy.
The teacher recorded her explanation like this:

$$13 \times 25 = \text{_____}$$

$$25 \times 10 = 250$$
$$25 \times 3 = + 75$$
$$\overline{ 325}$$

$$13 \times 25 = \text{_____}$$

$$13 \times 25 = 13 \times 100 \div 4$$
$$= 1300 \div 4$$
$$= 325$$

Solve the problems below. Record your explanation on paper.

1. 16 × 25 = _____

2. 8 × 25 = _____

3. 17 × 25 = _____

4. 22 × 25 = _____

5. 11 × 25 = _____

6. 52 × 25 = _____

What's a Good Estimate?
Greater Than, Less Than

Build your estimation skills. For each problem, tell if the answer will be less than (<) or greater than (>) the estimate given. Explain why you think so.

1. 127,203 + 162,887 is _____ than 300,000 because _____

_____

2. 32,782 − 22,765 is _____ than 10,000 because _____

_____

3. 42 × 28 is _____ than 1500 because _____

_____

4. $3\frac{2}{3} + 5\frac{5}{6}$ is _____ than 9 because _____

_____

5. $\frac{2}{5} \times 238$ is _____ than 100 because _____

_____

Now, make up your own problem like one on this page.

Name _____

Around Lake Tessa

This map shows Lake Tessa, White River, and some nearby towns.

Fill in the bubble next to the correct answer.

1. What are the coordinates of Mt. Hope on this map?

○ **A.** (2, 6) ○ **C.** (2,0)
○ **B.** (6, 2) ○ **D.** (6, 0)

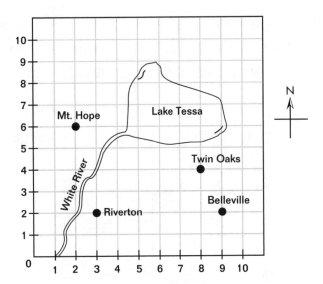

2. Each square unit represents one square mile. Which is the best estimate of the surface area of Lake Tessa?

○ **A.** 8 square miles
○ **B.** 10 square miles
○ **C.** 12 square miles
○ **D.** 14 square miles

3. Which list shows the towns in order according to how close they are to the shores of Lake Tessa?

○ **A.** Mt. Hope, Riverton, Twin Oaks, Belleville
○ **B.** Twin Oaks, Belleville, Mt. Hope, Riverton
○ **C.** Mt. Hope, Twin Oaks, Belleville, Riverton
○ **D.** Twin Oaks, Mt. Hope, Belleville, Riverton

4. Mrs. Sanchez lives in Mt. Hope. She works in Twin Oaks from Monday to Friday. If a bridge is built across White River near Lake Tessa, it will save her 5 miles of driving each work day. How many miles less will she drive in 50 weeks?

○ **A.** 10 miles ○ **C.** 250 miles
○ **B.** 25 miles ○ **D.** 2500 miles

5. One-half of the triangular area between Riverton, Twin Oaks, and Belleville is forest. Which is the best estimate of the forest area?

○ **A.** 2 square miles
○ **B.** 3 square miles
○ **C.** 6 square miles
○ **D.** 12 square miles

The World's Largest Islands

Phil made a poster of the six largest islands in the world. Unfortunately, 5 of his six labels fell off. The other five labels are Baffin Island, Borneo, Madagascar, New Guinea, and Sumatra.

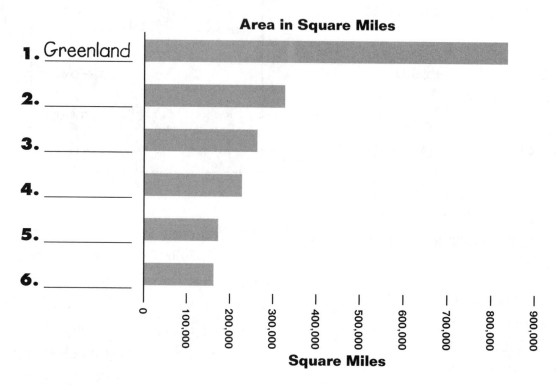

Area in Square Miles

1. Greenland
2. _____
3. _____
4. _____
5. _____
6. _____

Square Miles

1. Greenland has an area of 839,999 square miles. Write the word name for this number.

2. The area of Madagascar is 226,657 square miles. What number place on the chart belongs to Madagascar?

3. Baffin Island is only about 1000 square miles larger than Sumatra. What place on the chart belongs to Baffin Island?

4. Which position on the chart belongs to New Guinea if it has more than 300,000 square miles?

5. If Phil picks up one of the five dropped labels without looking, which letter is the name most likely to begin with? What is the probability that the name will begin with this letter?

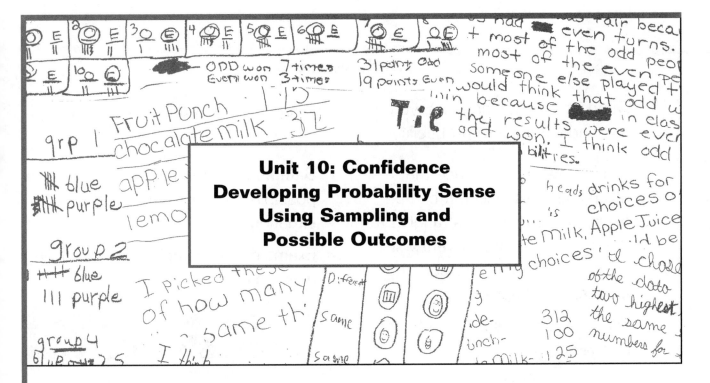

Thinking Questions

If a bag contains cubes that are either red, blue, yellow, or green, can you predict the number of red cubes in the bag based on a sample? What are all the possible outcomes of rolling two dice?

Investigations

In this MathLand unit, you will develop probability sense, using sampling and possible outcomes. You will investigate how sampling can be helpful in making a prediction, and you will learn how to make your predictions more accurate. You will also explore sample spaces and use them to determine whether a game is fair or not.

Real-World Math

Notice how often people make decisions based on predictions of future events. When it is not possible to know all the data, decisions are made based on past experiences. Spacecraft launch dates are chosen based on past weather patterns. When do you make decisions based on the probability of an event occurring?

Math Vocabulary

During this MathLand unit, you may be using some of these words as you talk and write about probability.

Probability is the chance that a given event will occur. It can be expressed as numbers ranging from 0 (no chance that an event will happen) to 1 (absolute certainty that an event will happen).

Example: There is a 50% chance of showers today.

You can make a **prediction** based on what you know or observe.

Example: It's very hot today. I predict that we will sell more drinks than soup.

Sampling is a technique used by investigators to predict what a larger group is like. A small proportion of a population or group is studied to make predictions about the whole group.

Sample space is the set of all possible outcomes in a given situation.

Example: The sample space of rolling a single die is shown below:

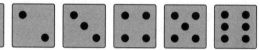

The **ratio** of two numbers *a* and *b* is *a* ÷ *b*, or *a/b*. It is sometimes written *a* : *b*.

Example: If the ratio of boys to girls in a class is 2 : 3, it means for every two boys there are three girls. In a group of 50 students, there would be 20 boys and 30 girls.

Proportionality is the concept that relationships keep the same ratio as quantities or amounts change.

Example: If three out of five apples from a tree have worms, then the logical conclusion would be that 30 out of 50 apples from that tree would have worms.

Name _____

Confidence Crossword

Use the clues and the words in the word bank to solve the word puzzle.
Unscramble the letters in the triangles and circles to figure out the answer.

Word Bank

- data
- predictability
- prediction
- probability
- proportionality
- ratio
- sampling
- sample space
- survey
- tally

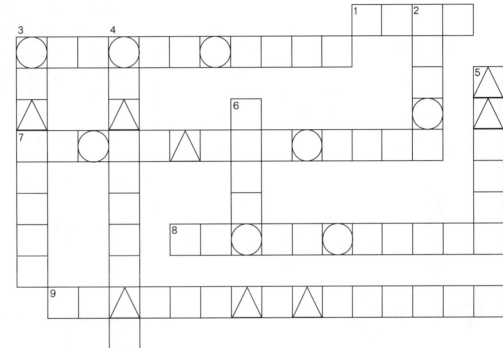

Across

1. facts and information
3. set of all possible outcomes
7. the extent to which something can be foreseen or predicted
8. the chance that an event will occur
9. keeping the same ratio as amounts change

Down

2. a mark representing a number
3. used to predict behavior of a larger group
4. guess based on what you know
5. way to gather data about a subject
6. sometimes written a : b

We take samples to predict

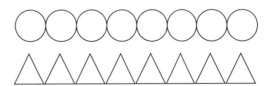

> ▼ **PARENT NOTE:**
> Talk with your child about times when you have made
> a prediction and about your basis for doing so.

© Creative Publications

Skill Power • 5 **213**

1

Find the Difference

$6881 - 5919 =$ _____

Explain your thinking.

2

Choose the Correct Answer

Cristin leaves college at 8:25 A.M. to go home. Her driving time is 5 h 14 min. She takes a 20-min lunch break and an 8-min rest break. What time does she arrive at home?

A   1:53 P.M.   C   2:03 P.M.

B   1:57 P.M.   D   2:07 P.M.

Explain how you know.

3

Macadamia Nuts

Jeff has $3.30 to spend on macadamia nuts. It costs $0.73 for $\frac{1}{4}$ lb of nuts. How many pounds can Jeff buy?

Tell how you know.

4

True or False?

The surface area of the Pacific Ocean is 64,186,300 sq mi. The Atlantic Ocean is 33,420,000 sq mi. True or false? The Pacific Ocean is close to twice the area of the Atlantic Ocean.

Explain your thinking.

1

Find the Product

$10.48 × 25 = _____

Show your thinking.

2

Choose the Correct Answer

Which is the answer for
1.1 − 0.73 = _____ ?

A   0.59

B   1.83

C   0.37

D   1.6

Explain how you know.

3

Marine Mammals

At the marine animal center there are 41 dolphins, seals, and sea lions. Two of the animals are dolphins. There are 9 more seals than sea lions. How many of each type of animal is there at the center?

Tell how you know.

4

True or False?

Fifty-seven fifth-grade students are going to the wildlife refuge. Each group can have no more than 4 students. Each group needs 1 adult. True or false? There will be 14 groups of students and 14 adults on the field trip.

Show your thinking.

1

Divide

$9\overline{)8396}$

Explain your thinking.

2

Choose the Correct Answer

Which is a true equation?

A $\frac{1}{2} - \frac{1}{16} + \frac{1}{4} = \frac{5}{8}$

B $\frac{2}{3} + \frac{1}{6} - \frac{5}{12} = \frac{5}{6}$

C $1\frac{7}{10} + \frac{2}{5} - \frac{9}{10} = \frac{1}{5}$

D $\frac{3}{10} + \frac{1}{5} + \frac{7}{10} = 1\frac{1}{5}$

Show how you know.

3

The Answer Is $\frac{1}{6}$

Write 6 subtraction equations that have this answer.

4

Newspaper Ads

Mrs. Hatfield wants to place an ad in the newspaper classified section. Each day she runs the ad it will cost her $6.96 for each line. She has a 2-line ad she wants to run for 4 d. How much will her ad cost all together?

Tell how you know.

Election Time

There are 500 students at Elmbrook School. Some of them took part in a survey. The survey asked whom students would vote for in an upcoming school election.

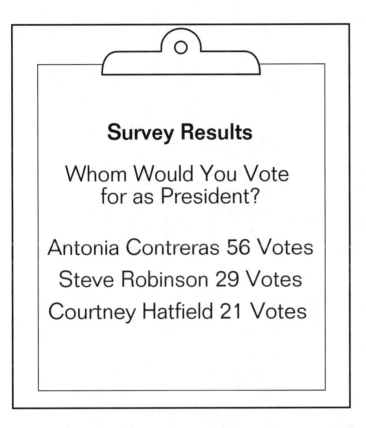

Survey Results

Whom Would You Vote
for as President?

Antonia Contreras 56 Votes

Steve Robinson 29 Votes

Courtney Hatfield 21 Votes

1. How many people took part in the survey?
2. About what fraction of the students at Elmbrook School took part in the survey?
3. Use the survey as a sample to give your predictions about the election outcome. Give as much detail as possible. Explain your thinking.

What's an Easy Way?
Computation Review

Solve these problems as quickly as you can. Use the strategies that work best for you.

Place <, >, or = in the circle to compare the numbers.

1. $\frac{1}{2}$ ◯ $\frac{1}{8}$

2. $\frac{3}{8}$ ◯ $\frac{1}{4}$

3. $\frac{10}{12}$ ◯ $\frac{5}{6}$

4. $\frac{3}{5}$ ◯ $\frac{2}{3}$

5. $\frac{2}{7}$ ◯ $\frac{2}{5}$

6. $\frac{3}{4}$ ◯ $\frac{5}{8}$

Multiply.

7. $\frac{1}{3} \times 27$

8. $\frac{3}{4} \times 16$

9. $\frac{4}{5} \times 40$

10. $\frac{2}{3} \times 33$

11. $\frac{4}{9} \times 45$

12. $\frac{7}{8} \times 56$

Solve.

13. $4568 + 1212$

14. $98{,}992 - 2889$

15. 6.7×5

16. $43.95 \div 5$

17. 2387×5

18. $4.56 + 27.8$

19. $65{,}223 - 6821$

20. $37.38 \div 6$

1

Write the Answer

621
× 24

Show your thinking.

2

Choose the Correct Answer

Which is the answer for
3268 ÷ 40 = _____ ?

A   80

B   80 R28

C   81 R28

D   81

Show your thinking.

3

What's the Better Deal?

A season pass to the amusement park costs $45. A 1-day pass costs $16.95. It is possible to get a $4 discount on a 1-day pass. When is a season pass the better deal?

Explain your thinking.

4

True or False?

(Hint: One gal of water weighs 8.33 lb.)

15 gal of water weigh 124.95 lb

5 gal of water weigh 41.65 lb

$\frac{1}{2}$ gal of water weighs 16.66 lb

If any statements are false, change them to make true statements.

1

Find the Sum

14,720
+ 8,585

Show your thinking.

2

Choose the Best Answer

Mr. Olsen bought $17\frac{1}{3}$ sq yd of carpet for his bedroom. The carpet cost $21 a square yard. How much did the carpet cost?

A   Exactly $323.40

B   About $300.00

C   About $360.00

D   Exactly $362.33

Tell how you know.

3

Party Time!

All the fifth-grade classes are having an end-of-year party. There are 142 fifth graders and 4 teachers. How many packages of paper plates, cups, and napkins do they need? The plates come 24 to a package, cups have 60 in a package, and napkins have 120 in a package.

Explain your thinking.

4

True or False?

Juice will be served at the party for 146 people. A carton of juice serves 16 people. True or false? They will need 9 cartons of juice.

Show how you know.

Name _____

Find the Quotient

$18 \overline{)726}$

Show your thinking.

Choose the Correct Answer

Which has an answer of $1\frac{5}{8}$?

A $1\frac{7}{8} - 1\frac{1}{4} =$ _____

B $3\frac{3}{8} - 2\frac{3}{4} =$ _____

C $2\frac{1}{4} - \frac{5}{8} =$ _____

D $1\frac{3}{16} + \frac{5}{16} =$ _____

Tell how you know.

The Answer Is 128

Write 3 multiplication equations that have this answer. Each equation should have at least 3 factors.

Agree or Disagree?

Shereen read on the bread label that a slice of bread weighs 25 g. There are 18 slices of bread in the loaf. She said the loaf weighs a total of 453 g. Do you agree or disagree with Shereen?

Explain your thinking.

Time for Lunch!

Pico's Pizza has a lunch special. They ran an advertisement about their special in the local newspaper. Do you agree or disagree with their advertisement? Explain your thinking.

Try Pico's Pizza Lunch Special

Choose one topping, one type of cheese, one sauce.

Over 36 different pizzas!

Only $4.99—includes our house salad!

TOPPINGS

Mushrooms
Sausage
Pepperoni
Ham
Bell Peppers
Tomatoes
Olives
Red Onions

CHEESE

Mozzarella
Ricotta

SAUCE

Tomato
Pesto

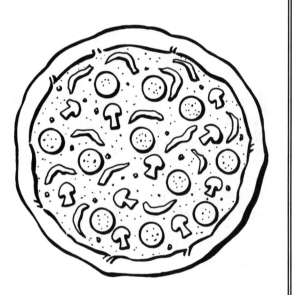

What's Your Strategy?
Convince Me!

Name _____

John and Sandy solved the problem 438 ÷ 15 = _____ . Look at their solutions. Notice that John and Sandy got the same, correct answer, but they used different strategies.

John explained his strategy.
The teacher recorded it for the class like this:

Sandy used a different strategy.
The teacher recorded her explanation like this:

$$438 \div 15 = \text{_____}$$

$$15 \times 20 = 300$$
$$438$$
$$-\,300 \quad 20 \times 15$$
$$\overline{138}$$
$$15 \times 4 = 60$$

$$138$$
$$\underline{-120} \quad 8 \times 15$$
$$18$$
$$\underline{-15} \quad 1 \times 15$$
$$3$$
$$20 + 8 + 1 =$$
$$29 \; R \; 3$$

$$438 \div 15 = \text{_____}$$

$$450 \div 15 = 30$$
$$50 - 38 = 12, \text{ so } 438 \div 15$$
must be 29 with a
remainder.
$$450 - 15 = 435,$$
$$438 - 435 = 3,$$
So, $438 \div 15 = 29 \; R \; 3$

Solve the problems below. Record your explanation on paper.

1. 123 ÷ 12 = _____

2. 558 ÷ 8 = _____

3. 809 ÷ 9 = _____

4. 1199 ÷ 12 = _____

5. 457 ÷ 5 = _____

6. 297 ÷ 6 = _____

▼ **PARENT NOTE:**
Students often add or multiply to find the answer to a division problem. Their explanations may show good reasoning skills and a step-by-step approach.

Name _____

A Block Pattern

Blocks are arranged in a pattern as shown:

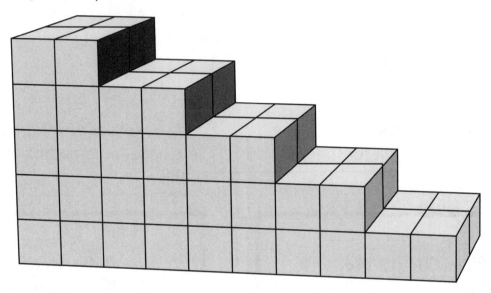

Fill in the bubble next to the correct answer.

1. How many blocks are there in all?

  ○ **A.** 30   ○ **C.** 50

  ○ **B.** 40   ○ **D.** 60

2. Suppose the blocks are glued together. How many blocks are only glued together on two sides?

  ○ **A.** 0   ○ **C.** 10

  ○ **B.** 2   ○ **D.** 12

3. What fraction of the blocks are in the top two layers?

  ○ **A.** $\frac{1}{5}$ ○ **C.** $\frac{3}{5}$

  ○ **B.** $\frac{2}{5}$ ○ **D.** $\frac{4}{15}$

4. All square faces on the top and the four sides of the arrangement must be painted. How many squares in all will be painted?

  ○ **A.** 60   ○ **C.** 100

  ○ **B.** 160   ○ **D.** 200

5. If the pattern is continued, how many blocks are needed for a row of blocks under the pattern?

  ○ **A.** 11   ○ **C.** 24

  ○ **B.** 12   ○ **D.** 30

▼**PARENT NOTE:**
The problems on this page give students practice in answering questions about patterns and predictability. It also prepares them for the format they may see in a testing situation.

U.S. Population

This graph shows how the population of the United States has changed over the past 100 years.

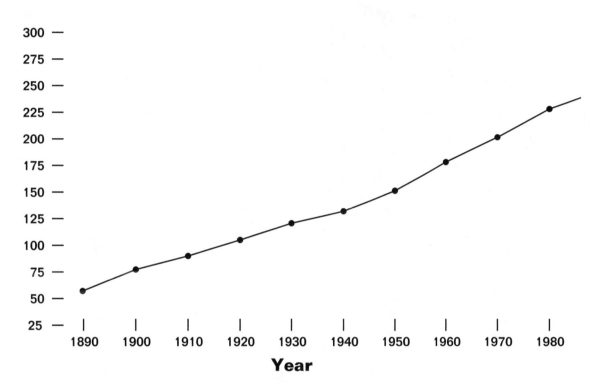

1. In which year was the population about 150 million people?

2. Estimate the population in the year 2000.

3. In which year was the population about twice the population in 1920?

4. The years shown on the graph are called census years. What are the next three census years after 1990?

5. For a school census, 12,000 surveys were sent to homes in the school district. $\frac{3}{5}$ of the surveys were answered. How many surveys were answered?